Other-Dimensional Entities

THEIR RECOGNITION & RELEASE

Christopher Freeland

PREFACE BY RICHARD GROSSINGER

© 2022 Christopher Freeland. All rights reserved. Any unauthorized use of this publication is prohibited by law. No part of this publication may be reproduced or transmitted in any form or by any means, electronic or mechanical, including photocopying, recording, or any information storage and retrieval system for public and/or private use without permission in writing from the publisher.
ISBN: 9781916159709

Dedicated to Boa Diya

In deep Gratitude
for your mercy and science

Contents

PREFACE 5
INTRODUCTION 9
CHAPTER 1 A SUPERIOR INTELLIGENCE 15
CHAPTER 2 SENSES 19
CHAPTER 3 ENTITIES IN OTHER CULTURES 31
CHAPTER 4 OTHER DIMENSIONAL ENTITY
MANIFESTATION 45
CHAPTER 5 ALTERNATIVE RELEASE PROCESSES 49
CHAPTER 6 PLAIN VANILLA POSSESSION AND COMMON
OR GARDEN OBSESSION 55
CHAPTER 7 SOLITUDE OR COMMUNAL LIVING 61
CHAPTER 8 BLACK MAGIC 67
CHAPTER 9 CURSE 77
CHAPTER 10 METHOD OF ANALYSIS 81
CHAPTER 11 TEXTUAL AUTHORITY 87
CHAPTER 12 DEALING WITH THE OTHER DIMENSIONAL
ENTITY PHENOMENON 95
CHAPTER 13 EASY RECOGNITION 101
CHAPTER 14 PERMISSION & ATTITUDE 105
CHAPTER 15 PROTECTION 109
CHAPTER 16 HISTORIC CHARACTERS SHOWING OTHER
DIMENSIONAL ENTITY PRESENCE 115
CHAPTER 17 MISCELLANEA 119
CONCLUSION 122
Appendix 1 124

PREFACE

We who currently dwell in the material world have become addicted to its phenomenology, so we experience it as the supreme and only reality. Understandably in an age of materialism as the world religion, people ascribe all causes and effects to their new God: the Algorithm. They view circumstances as purely circumstantial while discounting entities living in their experience of other dimensions and frequencies. Christopher Freeland in his youth was a British Gurkha officer, then a guide on photographic safaris in Zambia, then a more psychic sort of guide in Burma and Thailand. His career was as a French-to-English translator with a skill set in nuclear-generated electricity and telecoms, but he has a Clark-Kent-like second identity as a dimension-to-dimension translator of more consequential karmic energies and transmissions. Some might call Freeland an "exorcist," but he does not exorcise — kick out or try to vanquish — lost or unhealthily attached spirits; instead, he is a psychopomp and Paladin who tries to guide them where they need to go next, into their own light, away from the souls they are troubling. His own training in Vedanta makes him less dualistic and more broadly compassionate than a Vatican exorcist concerned mainly with myrmidons of Satan and protecting against invasions of evil. For Freeland, proper communication with entities entails putting them at peace as well as bringing relief to their attachees.

If, as Freeland presumes, sixty percent of all humans are possessed with disembodied entities, this is a critical service for not only individuals' mental health but for civilization as a whole. Attached spirits, without the natural visas of bodies that allow them to travel here, use oft-harmful expediencies to try to affect changes and fix wrongs from their lifetimes in a material world. The degree of emotional disturbance and sheer vandalism, violence, and idle mischief in the world cries out for people to recognize spirits in distress and help them understand their situation, the transitional nature of all life, and move into their next sphere of identity.

Freeland's techniques and adventures, as chronicled in this book, give readers a different way of looking at their dilemmas as well as the beginnings of a manual for addressing and dissolving spirit attachment. Freeland has developed "spirit radar" and an *ad hoc* tool kit from his studies and practices across Eurasia; he shares these generously with his readers. If nothing else is learned from reading *Other-Dimensional Entities,* one can begin to train a perception that other dimensions comprise a senior realm to which the so-called living are the junior partner. The paradox is that *ODE* will put you more solidly and poignantly in your own body, attuned to the beauty and exquisite harmonies of this dimension because it frames your existence in a multiverse of life, molting entities, and their agencies and volitions rather than in a dead, nihilistic accident of molecules, fire, and dust. In taking Freeland's tour through the spirit stratosphere and ionosphere, you will appreciate the sound of rain and the scent of a hyacinth: the wonder of life in our "densosphere."

There are some particularly exquisite teachings in this book as well as an introduction to the magic of radiesthesia. With the confidence and wisdom of a master, Freeland spells out the nature of passage between this world and the next bardo realm, offers thanatological landmarks and advice, which is especially crucial for those convinced of the singular reality of the material world. People in passage need to know how to connect one form of consciousness to another, to go toward their own essential being, and to accept the ways of navigation and well-intentioned hellos—extended ghost hands and calls—of benign and helpful beings. *Other-Dimensional Entities* is, in effect, a mini-Vedantic Book of the Dead, a mind yoga taught by a yogi.

Freeland specifies light as not just an electromagnetic phenomenon of the sort he translated between French and English but "a luminous aspect of our intimate reality." Both "lights" are light in their own spheres, but photons are particles that turn into light, whereas consciousness or soul light is a *source* luminosity that gives rises to particles and all things. I am reminded of a prayer that commune dwellers at Lama Foundation in New Mexico chanted to the starry heavens in the 1960s: *"Praise God for the Light Within Me, / Praise God, let love abide."* That mantra had a slight hiatus, a tonal dip between "with" and "in," that carried the unique vibration of personal reality: radiance, illuminescence, light.

Source luminosity allows him to introduce wireless energy and interdimensional telecoms. Someone with both a deep understanding of machines that send electrical pulses and Vedantic training is able to recognize and develop devices that operate between dimensions.

Preface

Telecommunications, WiFi, the internet, cell phones, and various degrees of generational broadband—4G, 5G, 6G—whatever your opinion or philosophy (technocrat or Luddite) were discovered and developed in *this* dimension only because they have corresponding forms for *inter*dimensional communication. That is where radionic devices come in. They have "wires," but these are sigils and runes, not metals or wires. They send and receive other-dimensional energy, not electrons. They also have value as screens and shields, much like Faraday cages or lightning rods. Instead of being run like phone lines, motherboards, and printed circuits, radionic means are esoterically drawn like sacred geometry in grid form, hieroglyphed, and alchemically purposed to intercept and transmit clairsentiently between our visible material world and its imperceptible aura. These bracelets, rings, coins, and medallions look like the guts of an old portable radio, but the stations they receive are inaudible but clairaudient. An Italian note from my 2006 travel journal describes radionics in the underground temple of Damanhur, near Turin, and places it in a broader cosmic context. Falco was Damanhur's founder, who claimed to be an interstellar as well as an interdimensional traveller and to have brought selfic technology from another solar system:

"A super-alchemy runs the Damanhur complex, Falco's informally branded selfic technology, culminating in an operating hermetic city as might have been pictured by Pico della Mirandola or Robert Fludd. Falco uses the word "selfic" instead of "radionic." Radionics is a discredited nineteenth-century meta-science for transmitting energies through grids and geometries and for healing at a distance. It generates a kind of metaphysical electricity that does not require direct electronic contact. Falco intends something slightly more discrete: the release of the intelligent alchemical properties of metals for transmission of energies across dimensions without reference to limitations of relativity, ordinary terrestrial currency, or the speed of light. In this cosmology, metals are given to humans primordially and purely and archetypally as devices that can be converted to spiritual transmission but thus far have been used at large only to imbed a lesser secular technology into the molecular memory provided by each distinct metal's intrinsic shape—e.g., its capacity to hold form and transmit primitive kinetics in the download of electricity and magnetism. What is crucial to the Damanhurian belief system is that all metals are *also* individually intelligent in another, more animistic way at a level that has not yet been discovered by mankind as a whole. One does not have to run voltage through them to get them to transmit information and force.

"We as a civilization and a world (among the many worlds) have missed the point. We have lost the operating manual inside our own planet and inside our beings for our planet. Thus alienated, we are running a minor gas station when living alchemical theater and free-energy technology are close at hand."

Another topic that Freeland aces is the distinction between Hinduism and Buddhism. In a time of popularized Buddhism, many people do not realize that, in Buddha's legacy, there is no surviving individual soul; there are no forms of Buddhist practice that lead to becoming a transdimensional entity. Everything has impermanent, conditioned existence and dissipates into its essential nullity on death. It cannot reincarnate or find a bridge to another entity. There is no equivalent to the Hindu Atman or soul-spirit. Freeland, as an ordained Vedantic swami, understands consciousness as present in all states and as multiple forms and potentialities simultaneously. His work with other-dimensional entities is an extension of his Vedantic view of nature.

One of the more sustaining features of this book is the author's profound conviction that universal materiality is a delusion. This conviction is so lived, earned, and dead-reckoned that he transfers it to the reader like a psychosomatic medicine or Buddhist *terma* (hidden treasure). He says, "My total conviction is that if we do not relate to what we truly are, we will spend our lives in delusion. That is no idle opinion or judgement, merely a quiet, unshaken confidence that I, as a human entity, am a spark of this Superior Intelligence, therefore no different from it intrinsically. Our egoity and belief that we are physical entities lead us away from that absolute truth."

That is the real basis of his valuable syllabus, not ghost-busting, not even metempsychosis, not demonology or voodoo, but a recognition of the big picture, a universe of illumination, spirit, mystery, and hope.

Richard Grossinger, author of *Bottoming Out the Universe: Why There Is Something Rather Than Nothing* and *Dreamtimes and Thoughtforms: Cosmogenesis from the Big Bang to Octopus and Crow Intelligence to UFOs*.

INTRODUCTION

My total conviction is that if we do not relate to what we truly are, we will spend our lives in delusion. That is no idle opinion or judgement, merely a quiet, unshaken confidence that I, albeit in the form of a man, am a spark of a Superior Intelligence, therefore no different from it intrinsically. Our egoity and belief that we are physical entities lead us away from that absolute truth, and result in the complexity we refer to as the world.

I claim to know no more nor less than the next person, but unlike the majority of my fellow humans, most of my life has been spent studying and investigating the nature of how that paragon of intelligent existence enables each and every one of us to experience our reality, whether individual or communal, all the while allowing a constant access to that apparent delusion, without which paradoxically, in the final analysis, we would not be able to recognize our true spiritual nature.

This last statement is essential to the subject matter of this pamphlet, for it concerns the make-up of Nature's creation, specifically the human element, and even more particularly, the 'spirit' component.

Forgive me if you will but it now seems important to introduce myself, for you are probably beginning to question my authority, even more earnestly, my authenticity.

Born in June 1949, raised in England, and according to the custom of those post-war years for the social group I was born into, sent to boarding school at the age of six. After leaving the army at the age of 21, with three years as an officer in the British Gurkhas behind me, I travelled overland to southern Africa. While working as a guide on photographic safaris on foot in the Luangwa Valley in Zambia, I was fortunate enough to encounter someone who was able to answer a key metaphysical question, which had been plaguing me since the age of fifteen. Swami Pranav Tirtha, a *dashnami sannyasin*, took me under his wing for eighteen months, until such time that he was satisfied that I met the criteria of initiation, and he ordained me as a monk with the name of Swami Chidananda Tirtha in May 1973, and sent me on my way to live whatever life had in store.

The philosophical system as propounded by Shankara is known as *kevaladvaita*, absolute non-dualism, which maintains that there is no difference of the soul from Brahman, Pure Consciousness or the totality. A subject that cannot be defined easily in a single paragraph, but as far as the system is concerned, requires intense study in order for it to become truly a way of being. This provided the basis of my spiritual understanding which continues to this day. All that took place from the age of twenty-two and I spent a total of four years living as a monk in India and Africa.

It was the time to absorb slowly the immense wisdom presented by the anonymous teachings of an ancient culture, and the unique Vedanta's teaching is the science of reality. It was a unique period affording me the leisure and luxury to search the intricacies of life and death, and much in between, forming the basis for a lifelong enquiry into the multi-faceted aspects of life. An exceptional experience because it allowed me to frequent some extraordinary people, including some of the weirdest specimens of Hindu society – the *nagas*, soldiers of the *dashnami sannyasins*, as well as the most erudite and compassionate of monks who took kind care of my physical and metaphysical wellbeing.

This was a period of intense training in the monastic disciplines of contemplation, meditation and study, primarily of the Vedantic triad of the Upanisads, the Bhagavad Gita and the Brahma Sutras. Occasion arose to make two additions to the curriculum in the form of Ayurveda, the Hindu medical system. This was in the company of Himatlal Trivedi, a splendid *vaidraj* (practitioner) who had the uncanny ability to tell a person exactly what they had eaten for their last two meals, such was his power of observation. I accompanied him in India and Africa in his practice amongst English and Gujerati-speaking patients. Thanks to his guidance and study of the Hindu medical classics (Caraka Samhita, Sushruta Samhita, Ashtanga Hrdaya), plus considerable experimentation of fasting and dietary regime on myself, I learnt a practical form of this medical art form.

The second addition was *Nyaya*, logical argument. The Hindu system of logic and debate, which proved to be an excellent way to consolidate understanding, with its emphasis on structure and rationality. Naturally, this effort involved a substantial amount of reading, much of which in the original Sanskrit so as to strive for the

Introduction

authentic essence, and avoid the inevitable linguistic bias introduced by translation. This last exercise was to stand me in good stead for my future professional career in France as a technical French to English translator specialized in a variety of modern technologies including nuclear-generated electricity and telecoms.

Curiosity has led me to cast the net far and wide in a search for solutions to the conditions we experience, and opportunity has allowed me the time and leisure to study and practice a range of therapies, including Traditional Chinese Medicine. Whilst living in France, I studied for a year with a French acupuncturist, who was persuaded to come out of retirement to teach Traditional Chinese Medicine (TCM) again. That grounding was then followed by many years of studying the Chinese classics: the Lingshu, the Huainanzi, the Suwen, along with in-depth reading of Soulié de Morant, Claude Larre and Elisabeth Rochat de la Vallée, in addition to extensive practice of moxibustion and acupressure. Whilst living in Chiang Mai, the opportunity arose to learn and practice a form of bio-energetics which involved a lot of practical moxibustion. The outcome of my studies of TCM affords a certain ease with this very complete approach to the human condition, which I practice using moxibustion rather than needling.

Those therapies include: the laying on of hands or magnetism, and use of magnets; radionics and medical dowsing; sound and colour therapy; the use of essential oils, Bach, Schussler and Amazon remedies; homeopathics, especially colloidal metals; bio-circuits and Realaxation – a series of postures allowing someone to move out of the sympathetic into the parasympathetic nervous mode by means of muscular stretching. Above all and for the purpose of diagnosis, rather Q&A, the pendulum is my tool of preference, as it can be used by one person alone, rather than with two people for muscle-testing or the bi-digital O-ring test.

I recount all the above because it is very pertinent to the origin of the subject of this book, over time the wholistic approach to finding a way to help a suffering individual turned out to be lacking somehow. The *vis medicatrix naturae* (the healing power of Nature), that elusive yet essential element is not always available. The discovery, basically, of the complexity of human affairs, obvious in all probability to a therapist of a native tradition, led me to try for a more in-depth look at a neglected psychic aspect of the human makeup. The purpose of this text, therefore, is to examine inasmuch as is possible the proposition that the spiritual dimension is as equally important as the physical, emotional, nervous and mental aspects, but totally neglected for lack of guidelines and apparent remedy.

So, the idea is to set out some concepts as to how that might impact our lives as a function of our understanding of those various cultural traditions, and in support of the practical method I relate some personal experiences as illustration.

Richard Grossinger, who has very kindly written a Preface to this essay, raised a while ago a most important point from the publishing standpoint, the text is lacking a core, so making it hard for the reader to relate to. Firstly, I am immensely grateful to Richard for marking these pages with his impeccable reputation, and doing me the honour of providing invaluable support. Secondly, I would like to try and reassure the reader by calling on your clemency, and indicate what I judge as the core. When we consider that we all – all that exists, and that doesn't – share a common core, a dimension that we pay little heed to, it is so present. As you can probably imagine, I am referring to our Self, which is never doubted but rarely investigated. It is such an essential component because it is us, even if we are incapable of recognizing it. That is the dimension we are familiar with, yet have absolutely no idea as to how it interacts or operates. That Self is my interpretation of the spirit that pervades one and all.

Well may you ask how is it that a human can claim to know about the spirit world. My humble answer backed by my core education as an orthodox Hindu monk in the Vedantic tradition would be, I do not know empirically, but such is my confidence, enhanced by years of experience, and confirmed to my satisfaction by answers to questions asked over the course of time, but especially of the entity to whom this essay is dedicated, that I know that we <u>are</u> also in the spirit world – a question of perspective. What is more, we have sufficient evidence from the past, with abundant literary sources in just about every tradition throughout the world, that there is clear indication of there being more than meets the physical eye. Even the Venerable Bede of England in the 8th century recounted a near-death story, and similar instances abound in recent history, sufficient to cast doubt and raise some questions whether we are on the right tracks. And that is what I propose here.

Where does one start an investigation of this nature? Let's take a look at what is available in the literary and cultural traditions, then place it in the crucible of experience.

Introduction

If you would keep one thing in mind when reading this essay, namely, it would be best that we never forget that there are multiple other forms of existence that we are constantly exchanging with – knowingly and otherwise. Most of those, or at least so it seems, are outside of and apart from us, but who is to say, perhaps even within our own bodies. What exactly is the soul we hear so much about, and the spirit? This is a zone of smoke and mirrors we are about to venture into, and in actual fact has always been there ever since we joined on being born. All I would ask you is to avoid that very human tendency which we all suffer from, of assuming that we humans with a body, mind and soul are the b-all and end-all of existence. There is more to the story than that.

Using inference, the absence of proof to the contrary, intuition and shared gnosis, there will hopefully arise a certain resonance with other souls, allowing for the quiet conviction that we are somehow or other interconnected, like the mycelia.

I believe it is what we loosely term 'spirit' that provides us with the glue for this connection, and we experience that association every time we admire a sunrise, receive a caring smile, or share any of the simple gestures that enhance our everyday existence. We can be forgiven for neglecting the logic of such values but not for hardening our hearts to them, for the only person we hurt by doing so is our very own self. It is commonly heard in this day and age that the only sin is to hurt someone deliberately, but how especially true that is, if it is yourself.

Why the title of this book Other Dimensional Entities? We are all entities, made up of all sorts of existing forms, for the most part invisible. It is, however, thanks to those invisible bits that we accomplish this amazing existence of life.

As with all of my other books the idea behind this slim volume is to share a little of what I have learned, this time about what we rather vulgarly call 'spirits'. My pretence even to write about this subject, considered taboo, mysterious, magical, spooky, sensational, scary, and what have you, knows no bounds, but because I fell into this line of business by 'accident', and now <u>know</u> it is an essential part of my phenomenal world, especially so as my task seems to be caring for others, it seems timely to offer a novel perspective in the hope that it might help provide some relief to those without a voice, and even a little guidance for those involved in release work.

Novel in that here you will find some practical, rather than mystical or mysterious, aspects to this subject drawn from ancient literary sources and years of experience, hopefully placing a stone that you can test and step on as the path slowly unfolds. We will, in all probability, never access the full picture in this existence, but sometimes we might have insights into these offbeat affairs, and for those of you interested or even operating in a similar line of work, it will be pertinent. Perhaps even to prepare those thinking of doing so, some ideas to mull over and help you find the right approach. For spirit release is not something to take on lightly, as it is not only surprising even when you believe you know what is what, but potentially deadly if you take on more than you can handle. And you will not necessarily know that until you are way out of your depth on this path of human alchemy from the material to the purely spiritual, so to speak.

Any serious search for reality has to deal with the simple question "Who am I?". Fascinating though it is, metaphysics is not the topic here, even if the 'spirit' component is the basis of the subject in this book. I assume that the reader has a sufficiently strong belief system that allows them to not question too much the reality, or at least the strong probability, of the existence of unseen presences or entities, which do and can alter not only our perception, but our behaviour, resulting in a vast range of experience, from a banal thought to life-extinguishing violence. Everything has a frequential aspect to its presence in this world, and sometimes we are able to access and even exchange with those things; as for example when buying your paper from the newsagent, or when seeing the relief in the eyes of the human whose plaguing demon has just exited to the light.

This essay is not a critique of religion, nor is it a call to philosophy. No theory or clever ideas as to what exactly death is, but simply a little cup of human kindness for those who have left their corporeal envelopes. There is very little available in any form of education to advise us about dying, how to do so without fear, what to expect, and how best to prepare ourselves for the only certainty that life holds.

So, gentle reader, here is my take on what could well be considered.

CF, Ballyieragh, 2022

CHAPTER 1
A SUPERIOR INTELLIGENCE

No matter the conviction, belief or understanding, you will probably agree that Nature and everything she comprises is governed by a superior intelligence which guarantees order and structure in the manifestation of life. Does that not infer a comprehensive interconnection that allows a very present sensation of awareness amongst all the beings included in, and perhaps beyond, that manifestation.

Apples grow on apple-trees and not elsewhere.

Quite what or how this force functions is beyond human grasp, for the extremely simple reason, we are an intimate part and parcel of the programme. We have no option but to accept that reality - irrespective of our curiosity and tendency to speculate. We do not possess the necessary ability to know – beyond a shadow of a doubt – how these matters work. However, insights are possible and that force is gracious, allowing us occasionally to communicate and interact not only with the life force itself, but also with the forms of existence (forms or entities) that I believe share our space as well.

To what extent we can put these insights into intelligible terms, accessible and acceptable by one and all, is another matter.

No matter what name we give to this organized force, we cannot ignore its utter control if we hope to achieve a wholistic view of existence and the potential human role therein. There is no question of defining this life force, but every reason to observe it and record for future reference the impact it has, as if one is painting a picture, rather than taking a photo.

This vital force is a silent, implacable, yet just quantity that ensures, from our viewpoint, that everything has its place and fulfils its purpose; such control is what is contested by people unable to accept our given place and want to assume a position of domination; those who in a seriously mistaken belief think they can direct phenomenal life and achieve what they want. Obviously, such autocratic humans who want to have things their way will not see it in that light.

From time immemorial, it would appear that humans in temporal authority, or in the process of attempting to gain such, have tried to abrogate and monopolize this force for their own nefarious ends. That is pure folly and arrogance, immensely damaging to the individual on that path, and definitely not of benefit to mankind, nor Nature at large. But, it is a distinct possibility as history so clearly shows and more so, it seems to me, now than at any other time in recent human history, fabricated pretentiously though it is to suit certain agendas, there is an urgent need to acknowledge and proclaim this Superior Intelligence because there is a concerted effort currently underway to foist the supremacy of artificial intelligence on humanity. Unless we are confidently decided on our reality, there is every chance that we fall for the propaganda and accept the ploy.

Our entire life is a story of navigation between what we believe and what we know, most of the time with the petty objective of accomplishing some desire or other. Sometimes we get it right, sometimes not, inevitably we suffer and cause suffering. Nowadays, it is fashionable to have an opinion on just about everything, even though we are fundamentally subject to nescience (not knowing), we are even encouraged to state that opinion based on what we are fed by the media and some unwritten right to express individual judgement, but opinion is judgement as of the time it is expressed.

That paradigm is a deliberate construct which makes us believe that we are aware. That is far from the truth, or we would remain in our integrity and be content with what we find WITHIN. This is where we have somehow been led astray, believing that the world is an independent, separate reality outside of ourselves, instead of knowing and experiencing the authentic reality of complete wholeness or unicity.

It might be useful and the right time to establish some notions which we can use as a foundation to help us gain as full a picture as possible. Using terms that hopefully everyone can relate to, while able to hang their own personal interpretation on them, we need to pass in review the various forms of being we encounter in our daily – and nightly – existence.

For all practical purposes, we know that the plain vanilla human is made of flesh and blood, an animating force and a bundle of impressions. We have some ideas as to how the physical works, although I would prefer the Chinese knowledge base if I wanted to gain a more comprehensive approach than the one offered by allopathy or modern western psychology, but cannot expect you to embrace that way of thinking just like that. Even on the emotional level, the inter-relationship between organ and emotion in the Chinese system is convincing and revealing of how dependent we are on the basics of what we eat and drink, and its assimilation in the environment in which we exist – we have a tendency to ignore such notions in our haste to satisfy our material "needs". Despite the seeming obscurity of the Chinese method, it is simple common sense, derived from lengthy observation of Nature. In an attempt to lighten these pages, I have relegated to the end the more academic and technical details for those of you who wish to read more of the relevant Chinese sources.

For the average denizen of the western world, the material world is pretty straightforward, one is born and one dies, end of story. This, however, is not to the satisfaction of many, we suspect, or even know that there is more to life, but who can help us? What is their authority? Are they authentic? Is there a hidden agenda? We have seen so much go down in the recent past, and perhaps wonder whether it has been going on for much longer, that we are no longer able to accept anything on face value.

If we are to keep it simple – which it is – we could do worse than take a look at what it is WE use to form what we then accept as truth. In other words, what we have learned to call the senses.

OTHER-DIMENSIONAL ENTITIES

CHAPTER 2
SENSES

There is no radiance without something to radiate

You might further agree that it would be a reasonable proposition with regard to a connection between the intangible and the manifest 'worlds', to consider the senses. If they do not form the actual bridge, then at least they form a major influence in the process which seemingly involves dealing with various dimensions, for lack of a better term. Most of us sense that there is more to the world than meets the eye.

There is a very useful Indian construct which speaks volumes on the erratic reliability of the sense we rely on the most, namely vision. When something comes into our range of vision, we say "This is such and such", for example in the glare of the noonday sun, a piece of mother of pearl is mistaken for silver, "This is silver" one concludes, however, on closer inspection the source of the illusion is found to be the shell, so one says, "This is a shell after all". 'This' is used on both occasions, firstly implying existence (of whatever it may be) and then identifying the object, first as the illusionary one and then, as what it really is when the object's true form is known. This 'this-ness' is the common aspect of all objects, it is of three types: 1/ that part of an object which is common to both the real object itself and to the illusion that arises in it as stated above; 2/ the true characteristics or part of the object which become manifest after disillusionment, which were not observed before, e.g. in the silver-nacre illusion, the triangular shape, the bluish back, etc. of the nacre which were not observed <u>then</u>, yet are special qualities of that particular object, as distinct from the general 'This'-ness; 3/ that imagined or illusionary quality prevalent during an illusion, which is only co-existent with the illusion.

The senses act as guides, faithful friends allowing access to dimensions where one can find the greater benefit, as a function of one's inherent tendencies. That would imply that we have more than the paltry five, a nonsense fed to us for the last two thousand, three hundred years.

Some human senses have a seat, so to speak, an apparent location in the body from where they operate, in that case we conveniently speak of a sense-organ. Consequently, it would be quite easy to appreciate Aristotle's haste in deciding that we have five senses on that basis (apart from his ongoing tussle with Democritus), but if it is true that where he went to school – for twenty years – in Egypt, there was apparently (the school of Kemit) a teaching whereby a human has 365 senses (unfortunately there seem to be no precise references in either the literature or epigraphic detail).

In our modern age, there have been some rather half-hearted efforts at revising this anomaly:

- Rudolf Steiner (1861-1925) put forward the opinion that humans enjoy twelve senses, in groups of three: (1) awareness of personality, awareness of thought, and balance; (2) sight, perception of the pattern of light, and temperature; (3) touch, perception of the pattern of movement, and hearing; and (4) smell, perception of sound, and taste.

- Michael J. Cohen, the eco-psychologist recently suggested 53 senses, his research and example are a credit to our species, especially with respect to Nature.

This author in his pamphlet, *Radiesthesia III, Senses*, attempts to enumerate the 365 Egyptian senses, which I would qualify as a little more than half-hearted. (What follows is drawn from that booklet).

If we are to break with the materialistic attitude which is the inevitable consequence of believing that we, as humans, have a mere five senses, it would be a shame to neglect the potential function listed in my treatise just because we do not have the approval of science as to their precise use and application or location.

In the same way that there are numerous body parts – pituitary, pineal, thymus, islets of Langerhans, etc. in the endocrine system, sensory neurons in the nerve ganglia, and so on – about which we have limited or no understanding. Do we cease all investigation just because some Greek decided a few thousand years ago that is how things are?

This obscure notion of there being only five senses has been consolidated over time. Perhaps even a perverse manipulation to encourage the human to believe that he or she is apart from the rest of Nature, a being that does not share the same environment as all other creatures; for that is one of the consequences of such an attitude.

We are even informed that we have lost the other senses, that is a myth. Like muscles which atrophy through lack of use, a sense might well suffer the same fate.

We humans are good at breaking things, and a lot of effort goes into that practice. Differentiation, the scientific practice of distinguishing between two or more things, by its very procedure does just that. So, in this effort at defining individual senses I am as guilty as everyone else, but with the simple difference that the thrust of my whole approach here is subsequently to integrate all the components, having applied my intuito-analytical ability, rather than leaving them separated. Even though those parts were never actually apart.

The first question we ought to ask with regard to the subject of the 'senses', could well be, how does one define a sense? It is evident that the so-called 'five senses' fall far short of the mark if we are speaking of the multiple capacities found in humans, animals and plants that allow us to make our way through life. So, throughout history, the scope has never been too well defined, and we are left to our own lame conclusions, instead of figuring out what they might be for, and how they could be maintained so as to serve their purpose.

That being so, and although there is little likelihood of achieving a definitive answer, it struck me that it could be useful to have a better understanding of the interface between our apparent 'inside' and 'outside'. We, as humans, all experience a life cycle every day of our lives, consisting of waking, dreaming and sleeping, a mutually dependent and essential sequence that takes place in what appears to be a commonly shared environment. Is it not possible that our 'senses' are the essence of that interface? Acting on that possibility, I set about trying to make a nomenclature. Of course, with a difference (it wouldn't be fun otherwise) using radiesthesia. To my knowledge, no one has ever attempted such while putting the findings to a test of veracity – which I would strongly recommend you do too.

OTHER-DIMENSIONAL ENTITIES

The hypothesis of 365 senses while intriguing in itself, is not the subject here and it might be best to limit the research to what I believe most relevant and pertinent to the question of the peregrinations of the human other dimensional entity.

1. Unicity

Foremost of the senses, or instincts, is the eternal – because it is incessant in all men, striving for unity. Forcing us to rise above the limitations of the phenomenal view, and despite repeated failure to, we cannot help returning to the attack, irrespective of the sneers of the materialist, who I suspect is subject to the occasional doubt. In theory, and for some in experience, it could be said to be the feeling of being-at-one, atonement if you like. By nature, it is a continuity; has there ever been any doubt in your mind whether you exist? The doubt is one of form, not foundation, giving rise to duality – me and you, and her offspring, multiplicity – the world. That sensation of oneness can never be affected. In none of the three states humans experience, viz. waking, dreaming and deep sleep, is that gnosis absent. But we tend to pass it by because we do not affirm its existence, and most of our socio-philosophical systems teach us to look outside for some form of governing influence, rather than applying introspection which would soon teach us that there is no inside nor outside. Its most common name is Love. It is much easier to love your neighbour, as we are told is the right thing to do, when you know you ARE your neighbour!

2. Consciousness

We are clearly confusing consciousness with "understanding," "awareness," and "thinking". There is a bad case of mistaken identity, or, more simply, the wrong nomenclature, which needs to be straightened out right from the very start, or we risk lapsing into the bad habit developed over our own life time and repeated through history. All this modern talk of consciousness, as in "a crisis of consciousness," "a need to raise consciousness," "transformation of consciousness," and so on, is due to a sloppily or inexactly defined term.

You might well agree that the nature of consciousness is "light," the main source of brilliance illuminating the senses, so allowing intelligence, inspiration, perception, cognition, and revelation. A substantially different beast from the electromagnetic and infrared frequencies supposedly from the sun which enlighten and enable our waking state.

Consciousness in the *Oxford English Dictionary* is considered to have several synonyms, awareness and wakefulness being among them. *Wakefulness* says it all, but do you hear the essential nuance of context that that word contains? It reveals about one-third of the truth. Just because there is consciousness in the waking state, does that mean it is the only state that consciousness illuminates? Definitely not, but that conclusion renders "consciousness" one of the most poorly understood terms of our epoch, a typical example of how treacherous language is.

So can we redefine Consciousness?

First, with a capital C, because it is the *only* one there is.

A good understanding of the term Consciousness is provided by nondualistic Vedanta (the confidential teachings of the Vedas as exposed by Shankara, *kevala advaita Vedanta*). This is as good a time as any to expand on that teaching for those not familiar with this unique standpoint.

There is a common belief that Eastern philosophy is about "becoming" one with the All. That may be so, but from the Vedantic viewpoint it would be a grave misconception, because there can be no question of becoming for the simple reason that you ARE ALREADY ONE WITH THE WHOLE. Due to ignorance or nescience of the true nature of yourself, however, you do not or choose not to see it. Ignorance is ignoring something once you know its nature, nescience is not knowing something; two very different beasts.

The very idea of trying to define Consciousness is one of those anomalies of human understanding. If we all have it and nothing can exist without it, how is it possible for a component part to define the whole? What's more, why is it necessary to limit it with words, as if it were something that could be measured? Such reasoning is radically opposed to its very nature.

Consciousness is limitless, one, omnipresent, all-embracing. In other words, a real whole shared by one and all, it cannot be differentiated by a category of species or protein (animal, vegetable, or mineral) or broken down into parts such as atoms, neutrons, or whatever; it defies classification whether divine, human, or mane, for the simple reason that it is the foundation and cause of all that exists. The downside of this is that Consciousness can be neither affirmed nor denied; reason can neither prove nor disprove it; it is not a subject of belief as a possibility, or rejection as an impossibility; and it is perfectly beyond the reach of mundane words.

The conviction of my own reality is intuition based; no one can dispute my Self. Even if they did, I would not be in the least affected — I know that I am. I employ the first person singular deliberately to emphasize the individual nature of this universal persuasion and would further argue that this holds true for every thing one encounters in this universe. However, if one were asked to prove the reality of anything other than one's own Self, one would insist on some very solid evidence and still likely remain sceptical.

Your own individual experience is called to witness here; you are not expected to adopt Hindu philosophical tenets, let alone adhere to what is written in the Upanishads now or in the future.

That we have lost the capacity/sense/knowhow to tune in, and stay tuned in to the world is in all likelihood the outcome of a combination of very human things - exaggerated egocentricity, the influence of materialism, or more specifically a belief in human superiority, and other similar addictions. It seems a reasonable supposition, in keeping with the individual intuitive experience, that we are in intimate connection not just with one another but with all that surrounds us, both animate and inanimate. But such a credo requires a quantum leap in understanding and a considerable humbling, because it means that you, as a human, are somehow on the same footing as the insect that just flew by, the unseen amoeba in your glass, or the distant mountain. It requires a progressive replacement of the ego — as the centre of your experiential subject-object world — as you gradually come to realize that in actual fact the ego never really existed as anything other than Consciousness.

It seems useful here to state my metaphysical understanding - I will keep it brief, don't worry. A number of life factors do not seem to change - a very important notion if we hope to gain an idea as to what life might be about. Simply stated, those factors are what we all, as humans, know. I.e. 1. We exist, no one can convince you otherwise, 2. We are conscious, more about Consciousness below, and 3. Every process, thought, action/reaction, originates from the common denominator of love or bliss, in other words, everything we do or think starts from the idea of achieving joy, a dim reflection of love which has no need for anything other than the oneness we all suspect underlies the whole.

Only from such an outlook, I believe, is one able to appreciate the nature of connection and possible communication that happens with the unrevealed entities we are discussing here.I would maintain that this is the source of happiness for one and all, being in balance with all in the environment.

The Nature of Consciousness

Duality and its immediate successor on the world stage, multiplicity, can be viewed as a consequence of the seeming appearance of differentiation, with truth disappearing like an ice cube in a glass of hot water, while the reality of unicity gives way to the usurper.

A brief explanation as to how Vedanta reaches this conclusion might be welcome for those not familiar with its methods. In passing, it is significant that there is no term in Sanskrit for the concept of matter, which might indicate the importance given to the material by the designers of the system.

Consciousness is, come hell or high water, present in all the states known to humans; it is ALWAYS there. Perhaps it could be expressed as the unqualified principle of gnosis (subject/object-free knowing), unobstructed by a subject (knower) or object (known) — the intuition that you are aware, able to perceive. Even renowned Buddhist, Mathieu Ricard, says in his useful book, *Happiness: A Guide to Developing Life's Most Important Skill*, "That faculty, that simple open presence, is what we may call pure consciousness, because it exists even in the absence of mental constructs." Of course that is not orthodox Buddhist teaching, for the simple reason consciousness is momentary for the proponents of Siddhartha Gautama, even though what he says is very true according to the common human experience.

In all likelihood, Consciousness is probably shared by everyone and everything around you, not just sentient beings. It is the intimate sensation that pervades all three states of waking, dreaming, and deep sleep. It has nothing whatsoever to do with the feelings caused by neurons or the nervous system, which, though of a material nature, need its total intimate support. Consciousness is omnipresent and all pervasive, requiring no input, although input cannot be perceived without it. Awareness is not Consciousness but cannot happen without Consciousness.

3. Awareness

Because of their intimacy, awareness is generally confused with consciousness. The definition of awareness requires an object to be aware of, therefore a *someone* to be aware of the *something*, and a context, as in not being aware due to the nonreceptivity of the senses. An adjectival consciousness if you will.

Awareness of something is the result of its perception by one of the sense organs. One can well imagine that this happens due to the agency of conjunction of perception and the object, which for both probably occurs thanks to Consciousness and some form of resonance or tuning. As Consciousness remains a constant without any need for a perceiving subject, object perceived, or conjunction of the two, it is also the raison d'être of existence and no different from it. Similarly, reality depends on Consciousness for its being, not on the way people think or behave. That is not, however, what we are taught.

Most of us experience life as a continuity of existence. We know, as in gnosis (or "intuit" if you prefer), only one thing throughout our entire earthly existence — "I am." Even when you awaken after sleeping well, you are convinced that it was you who slept and that the state abandoned prior to sleep resumes on waking. Some thing was there to witness the experience. This knowledge is an enduring companion and a most convincing one; what's more, it is consistently encountered in all the three states. Thanks to the constancy of Consciousness, we have a thread to our existence, and it is the only unchanging constant. Now there is something that deserves a moniker for itself, and that is the sense given to it and will be used here.

This "I am" thread, experienced while awake and in dreams, is undeniable. If you look back over the past, even if there have been immense transformations in your life, changes of personality perhaps, careers, companions, there is consistently the notion of "I" that runs as the underlying associate. Ultimately, this "I" is all we have to work on in a quest for the exact nature of our elusive individuality. Much has been written elsewhere on this subject, so this is probably repetition for many, but it nevertheless remains a fact of life. The "I" is here to stay for the duration.

It would seem very normal that this "I," being nothing other than Consciousness — the unique component shared by one and all — can assume aspects such as what we refer to as the conscious, subconscious, unconscious, or superconscious component of the mind for the simple reason that we are not truly familiar with its real, all-encompassing nature, and we need to express the apparent changes as a comparison with matters that correspond to what we believe we experience, know, and, of course being human, think we control. Such terms are merely adjectival to the principal noun, Consciousness.

From the very outset of our human life, we are easily duped into believing this "I" to be something other than what it truly is, as in the Hindu construct explained above. It starts out with the notion that "something is not quite right," a malaise that can assume huge proportions (even to a state of mental depression) if the call of the spiritual is denied. Refusal to listen to one's conscience, that inner voice that soon learns to keep quiet in view of the barrage of cerebral resistance opposing it, is a sign of the material gaining the upper hand. If one manages to maintain a balance of head and heart, there is a chance that much stress can be avoided. This state of object-less calm is harmony, so dear to all those on a serious quest for meaning to life.

With the passage of time, the effects of education, peer pressure, simple habit, and other factors, we learn mistakenly to assume the reality of the physical body as being a thing of constancy, with an increasingly vague notion of what "I am," or what is this mind thing that is somehow attached to me, and an even vaguer idea that spirit is involved in the overall picture. Yet all the while, we *know* that there is something more to life than the material body.

Consciousness is this inner thing, this voice that is especially familiar in childhood, in dreams, moments of intuition, meditation, that suggests there is more than meets the eye in our world, so influenced and even fabricated by intellectual reasoning and logic?

Awareness, the first step in differentiation as Consciousness moves, so to speak, into realms where we exteriorise and lose the centre.

These three form the backdrop of what would seem to be the basis whereby we perceive, receive and interact with external and internal stimuli, but awareness is the interface between the information conveyed by the sense and what, if any, action is taken.

4. Right

Moral considerations apart, humans have a distinct sense of what is right – for themselves, others and their surroundings. Perhaps more often encountered as a child – the voice of conscience – until such time that this inner voice is extinguished.

5. Wrong

Much the same idea as above.

6. Existence

We all know we exist – I hope so at least. But it is this very powerful sense of being which leads to the sense of awareness, mentioned above that in turn provides a sense of satisfaction, or love.

7. Love

There is nothing that is done in our human dimension that lacks this objective, which is very real, especially when not achieved. That is the driving force in any and every effort, love derives from the unity that underlies all. It is, however, a component of the Existence-Consciousness-Love triumvirate.

8. Nescience

An awareness that you do not know something which will either push you to find out and overcome the non-knowing, or remain in blissful ignorance – deliberate turning of a blind eye.

9. At ease or no tension

A sensation of comfort, the sensation of well-being, probably produced by the parasympathetic nervous modality.

10. Ill-at-ease or under tension

A sensation of discomfort, for whatever reason, caused by the sympathetic (fight-or-flight) nervous modality.

11. Communication

Interconnection could be a synonym for this ability. How many means of communicating with the outside world are there? They all probably use other senses or sense-organs to accomplish that task, such as eyes, speech, touch, ESP (it is extra because nobody bothered to write about how it actually works!), dream, telepathy, and so on. The bottom line is, nevertheless, that in an effort to re-establish the unicity of life, we inevitably revert to the harmony of Consciousness which is readily expressed through the immensely comfortable feeling when those lines of communication enabling connection with everything around us, are open.

12. Time

Not so commonly found in modern man as a sense per se, for the simple reason that time has become our governor rather than a collaborator which would be the case if man was to live closer to Nature. This is probably the most obscured sense, but the evidence is there that this sense is still with us. As for example when a person wakes just before or at the moment when the alarm clock is set; or knowing when to plant seeds because one is in sync with the moon.

13. Space

Here again, a sense that has been atrophied over the years due to non-application. It is experienced as a feeling of emptiness, the fact that there is nothing in your immediate surroundings that might be a threat to your well-being. It would perhaps be more correct to name it aether, for in the esoteric traditions, the aether has a faculty of connection and communication.

The thirteen senses listed above appear to be the most involved in this other dimensional entity affair. Forming the kernel of the human soul-spirit in its relations and communications with the environment. It would be foolhardy and presumptuous to try and fit together a scheme which governs how it works, that must no doubt remain a mystery, and what a magnificent and merciful construct.

The other 352 senses are not quite relevant here, so we will leave that rabbit hole for another time.

Obviously, we could not even envisage a spirit option without the material body which is seemingly only available to us in what we know as phenomenal life, and inversely, it is probable that only whilst in the human manifestation that we are able to contemplate the spiritual option, at least that is how it seems from the physical standpoint! At some stage in the dawning on our awareness of these options, there is a strong chance that we are going to choose one or the other. Not that one or the other is right or wrong, but as a matter of quiet conviction determined mostly by what it is one seeks for, and gradually learns. It

OTHER-DIMENSIONAL ENTITIES

might be rightly said that we have a restricted range of free will, and I would venture that it is fundamentally limited to whether we consider ourselves as spirit or physical beings, at least as regards what we then experience in life.

That attitude is going to colour one's whole outlook, and it would be worth remembering that may not be shared by one and all.

CHAPTER 3
ENTITIES IN OTHER CULTURES

Investigation in the 'spirit domain', as with so many other obscure aspects of life, at a certain stage has to rely on what you have personally experienced, because you know what you have sensed and no one can tell you otherwise, even though you may doubt the evidence, and with the passage of time, even the experience itself. All that goes to create a murky zone where what has not been said would imply that something is going on, which of course is not quite the reality most of us believe we all share.

There are some literary sources which are worth discovering, although their antiquity and foreign context makes them tricky to translate into terms we can comprehend and appreciate today.

Accounts of spirits and discarnate energy forms are to be found in most if not all ancient traditions. Such as with the Latins and their *manes,* referring to the entity left behind following the dissolution of the physical human body, the Hebrews have their *ob,* with various categories, *neshamah* or rational soul, *ruah,* sensitive soul, and even a vegetative soul, *nefesh,* (non-*nefesh* foetus and full-*nefesh* status discussed by Talmud commentator Rashi (1040-1105), incidentally gentiles are regarded as lacking *nefesh* status by orthodox Judaism!). The Egyptian soul had its *ren, ka, ba, Ib, sheut,* and *akh* but regrettably there is no definition as to what these might be. The Muslims have their *jinn,* with Mohammed even talking of the *ruh* although we need to refer to Avicenna to learn more of the impact spirits can have on humans. The Thai have their *phi (peta, am, chamob, ha, krahang, krasy, lok,*

OTHER-DIMENSIONAL ENTITIES

phrai, tai ha, thuk khun, khamod, nang tani, pa, ka, poang khang, hai, pob – the nastiest!).

You are beginning to understand perhaps how difficult it is to acquire any coherent scriptural understanding regarding this aspect of the human entity, despite the fact that there are apparently no cultures who neglect the phenomenon.

According to Chinese understanding of human make-up, common to both Daoism and Traditional Chinese Medicine, the idea developed, or solidified more than 2,500 years ago, that the human body encompassed two types of entities, usually described in English as "souls," which they call the *hun* and *po*. These two types of entities are associated by them with the *yang* and *yin*, respectively. The *po*, of which there are said to be seven, are of an earthly nature, being most closely allied with the flesh, so *yin*. The *hun*, of which there are said to be three, are of a heavenly nature, and *yang*.

The *hun* like the *shen* (pure spirit in its vital force form) originate from the heavens, and enter and exit the body through the *hun* gate (*hunmen*, acupuncture point BL47); upon death, they leave the body and return to the heavens. The Chinese practice of ancestor worship encompasses taking care of the departed *hun*, which, because of their residence in heaven, are thought to be able to help mediate the earthly human wishes with the gods. Further, it was thought that dissatisfied ancestral spirits (those who were not cared for by their offspring in succeeding generations) could cause illnesses or misfortunes.

Now while it is well beyond the scope of this booklet to develop Chinese cosmology, theory, or ways of life as written in the early texts, let's look at the workings of the human entity as portrayed in chapter 8 of the Lingshu, which offers a most detailed explanation of the functioning of life. The Huangdi Neijing (the yellow emperor's classic study of internal medicine) was believed to have been written at some stage during the Han Dynasty (206 BCE–220 CE); there are two sections, the Lingshu (spiritual core) being one of them, and as its name suggests it deals with affairs that can be loosely termed "the spiritual."

The idea is that life starts for animate beings when they are invested by an energetic force, an "energy" form, which for purposes of differentiation when dealing with human life goes by the name of *shen*, often translated as "spirit" in English, which of course creates further confusion in the mind of anyone who stops to think of the diversity of meanings given to that word. The term "heavenly input" might be a more appropriate translation because the Chinese characters can be reasonably interpreted as indicating "extending from heaven," but I will use the Chinese *shen* to avoid any misunderstanding.

The *shen* are cosmic forces, the spirits of heaven if you like, as opposed to *gui*, the spirits or ghosts of the earth; in the human, the former reside in the heart. The image of life is of heaven (*yang*) and earth (*yin*) in motion, with the influence of the sun and the cosmos coming from above and water rising from the earth, thus giving and animating life. Life exists when the essences combine with the breath of heaven and the creative force of the earth, giving rise to all beings. Life ends for all beings when those essences separate again and go back to where they originated from. The individual entity is formed of energy; that energy cannot be or manifest without a form, and that form cannot exist without the animating energy so clearly expressed in fire and water.

It does not seem unreasonable to propose that the function of *shen* is to guide and guard: to guide in the way of one's true nature (as in *dharma*) and accomplish one's life purpose; and to guard one's virtue or integrity in order to achieve that purpose.

So, the guides and angels we so often hear about in the new-age context could be seen as no different from these cosmic forces, minus the sensational effect of individual claims.

If one assumes that there is a physiological centre for such goings-on, as the Chinese system does, then it would most likely be the heart, which handles the unceasing movement of thought, action, and reaction. In its serenity and calm, it is the mirror of Tao (which I equate to the Hindu Consciousness), allowing all beings and things to exist, yet touched by none of them. When the heart is carried away by emotions and desires, which happens as we all know, matters get stirred up and harmony is lost.

There is a further very significant subcategorization of the *shen* spirits, specifically with regard to their function in the human entity and in relation to their earthly orientation. In this context we find the term *gui*, sometimes translated as "ghost."

- The hun, the yang component of gui, coming and going in relation with the heavens and therefore with qi, trend more toward the elevated aspects of activity requiring intelligence, knowledge, aspiration, imagination, and intuition.

The awareness, animating, and perceiving capacities of the human are ensured by the *hun* operating on the principles of movement and perception, and hence on understanding and the more physical aspects of sensation, emotion, knowledge, and thought. The *hun* reside in the liver and so are rooted in *yin*, although of a *yang* nature, thanks to the association with the heavens, and they bestow an animating quality to the blood.

- The po (residing in the lungs), the yin component from the earth, are associated with the more earthly metabolic functions of breathing, digestion, circulation, transformation, autonomic movements of human life, and, of course, creation. It does not seem unreasonable to suggest that the po are involved in the more basic instincts as we know them in the West, in the existential drives enabling the survival of all earthly species, namely: being, self-projection, interconnectedness, self-preservation, reproduction, sleep, and nourishment.

The combination and parting of *hun* and *po* are the origin of life and death in the human; keeping these two components in harmony is the way to ensure the life purpose. The *hun* and the *po*, animated by *qi*, allow the individual to live.

Ancient China can be counted on to provide a practical view, and from what I understand that is very much what they maintain whereby *De*, virtue, or the values which guide and support the way we behave, is the acme of our human effort. It is elegantly expressed in the Chinese character for virtue, made up of the following three components:

Chapter 3

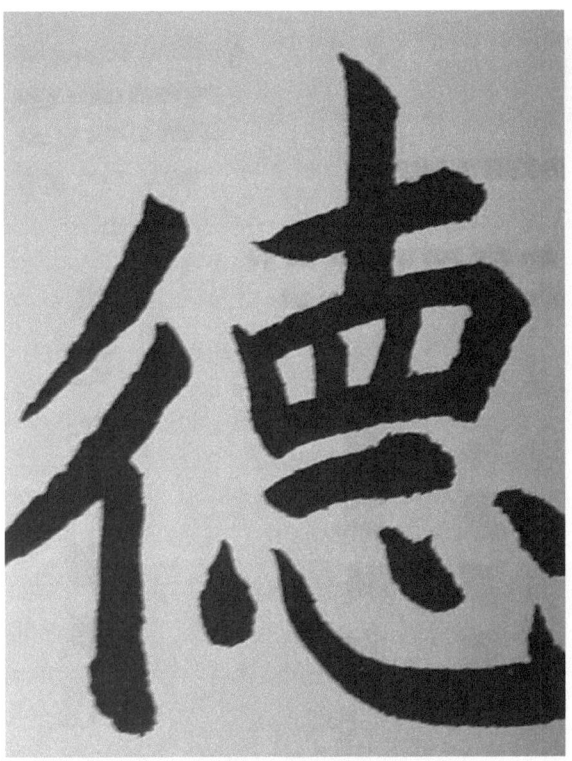

a/ the uprightness and b/ the authenticity of the heart as it moves on c/ its way. By means of virtue one is able to reveal and assume one's Self. Would that not be a truly worthwhile purpose of life?

Modernity in China, especially in the materialistic form of communism, has led us far afield from the ancient practice of Daoism. If we believe that we are a purely material entity, rather than spirit, we are incapable intellectually of fully considering the potential reality of a spirit dimension, let alone the totality of life. We only go half-way, paying lip-service to some vague sort of notion, resulting in a very incomplete understanding, which will contain its own shortcomings and deficiencies further hampering clear perception.

That is also the case with us moderns with Spiritualism and Spiritism (Allan Kardec made a system of it). Both of which, and especially the latter are an amalgam of mediumistic lore, Christianity, magic and psychology. They generally focus on the psychic (sensational) phenomena to attract interest, although practitioners such as John of God work the most extraordinary feats and miracles which cannot be lightly dismissed, they both encourage mediums to communicate with the 'spirit' world, and in John's case, to be completely invested by

OTHER-DIMENSIONAL ENTITIES

them, with strange consequences as we saw recently.

The dangers are clear in hindsight, as practitioners of both these systems have discovered but do not readily admit. The spirits who show up and manifest are often not quite what they seem, leading the gullible into mischief and fooling participants into irresponsible behaviour, causing irreparable damage and unpleasantness, but still the 'faithful' keep on encouraging the charade in the hope of some relief – which is found, but at what cost.

We operate in a very narrow field of conceptual understanding, and what could be more natural if we insist on believing that the only reality exists in the waking state. Most of the time, that understanding is also peer-influenced. However, as soon as we introduce concepts from other cultures or traditions, a degree of difference - generally exotic, if not mystical, is added. That may be of use, but most of the time it is not justified except to make up for one's own inability to simplify, along the lines maintained by Nature.

With regard to the phenomenal world, there would be little point going in to the conditioning and programming that allows the situation that we have today of outright materialism and the perverse form of materialistic spiritualism so common in this age. We know full well the density and the force of that education.

But if no one tells us who we are, or if we make no effort to go beyond the imposed belief that we are a physical entity with some vague notion – if we're lucky – that there is something more, such as a soul (whatever that is), with a bit of spirit thrown in for good measure, it is hardly surprising that we will flounder around till the end comes. That can only create an environment of confusion, disillusion and frustration, with no possible solution in sight, but suffering guaranteed.

Yet that is exactly what happens for the vast majority of people.

What is most pertinent here is to try and nail what these 'entities' can actually be and how, if at all possible, to relieve or remove them, so that some form of solace can be found – for all involved, not just the person suffering from their intrusion.

This last idea is most important in the clearance work that is involved. There are always several sides to a story, and that is equally so in the 'spirit' domain. The enquiry needs to be as all-inclusive as humanly possible, and then some!

We humans – at least the vast majority, and I would include 98% of the world (even in India) are not educated at all as regards the nature of spiritual matters, and the (apparent) interaction of spirit and matter.

Don't believe me – but please discover and intuit what you know, and once you've got to the very bottom of the sensation before drawing any conclusion, ask whether it fits in with an authentic, unadulterated ancient text, conform to what people worthy of trust have to say?

References in history, literature and the Bible are numerous and probably well known to you all, but I would add to this section a quote from Samuel Johnson: "I do not believe in spirits – I have seen too many of them."

I am personally very aware of (perhaps even with a certain aversion to) the sensational aspect which is so often attached to such notions, and prefer to remain in the domain of my own experiential knowledge base.

The traditional principles of learning in India are based on a tripod system, made up of three components: the preceptor principle, personal experience and scriptural authority. Together they provide an unshakeable foundation. If one's belief is based purely on one of those components, such as personal experience – as in Buddhism – without the support of the other two, failure is guaranteed, the base is far too shaky, standing on one leg only.

The preceptor principle is based, or should be, on the time-tested concepts of example, inspiration and clarity. The *guru* can be any form of life. Etymologically dating from the Rg Veda period, the Sanskrit word can be translated as 'heavy', as opposed to 'light-weight', a principle with which one associates steadfastness, solidity because it cannot be moved, and by extension (in Hindu thought), truth.

Obviously, the human species make the most practical teachers for us people, as conversation, teaching and example can be followed and practised. There is a wonderful example in Indian mythology of an adolescent, Dakshinamurti, (facing south in Sanskrit) seated in silence but with his hands in a specific mudra, as shown below (without the symbol Aum).

OTHER-DIMENSIONAL ENTITIES

The significance lies in the position of the fingers and thumb. The index finger symbolizes the ego, it is brought to the thumb, Brahman or the Superior Intelligence, while the other three fingers, representing the three qualities of nature, *tamas* illusion (middle finger), *rajas* activity (ring finger), and *sattva* spirituality (little finger), continue on their business.

The second leg of the tripod is personal experience. That can be a great teacher if one learns from the lessons accomplished. Which can only be achieved by constant witnessing of what passes through the mind. That is the core of the spiritual discipline, staying centred on the witnessing so that whenever a thought or emotion creeps in to the mind-space, you observe it, monitor it until it gives way to the next intruder of your interior calm. That is true meditation – witnessing – and it is an affair of 24/7.

When instruction and self-learning are corroborated by a text worthy of the faith, there forms a conviction based on intuition and reasoning. Doubt cannot shake that, although questioning is a natural and healthy reaction ensuring that one does not lapse into complacency.

Chapter 3

When we refer to and deploy all our senses, we are able to access domains unsuspected, in much the same way as we dream. In the dream world we are untrammelled by the physical restrictions and societal bonds which limit our faculties in the waking state.

The 'spirit world' as some kind of 'external' event is subject to interpretation and diverse opinion, and that is where the problem mainly lies, not in the actual existence of such a phenomenon, for that is only debatable from the narrow vision of the waking world, and an exclusively perceived material human condition. The first step on the path to virtue is recognising the fact that we are a combination of flesh, spirit and energy thanks to some marvellous alchemy worked, or at least apparently so, by that Superior Intelligence.

Whilst on the subject of vision, so long as we behave as physical humans, we restrict ourselves to a limited sensual capacity, with restricted magnetic field and range of electric current which determine the scope of that ability.

In much the same way that we perceive with our eyes only a minute spectrum of the Hertzian frequency range – from 400 to 750 nanometres – the visible electromagnetic range available to humans in the form of light, we are unable to 'see' if we only use our eyes. To put some perspective on this extremely limited range, it is enough to consider how some of our modern technologies employ those frequencies, for example: X-ray operates at between 10^{-7} and 10^{-12} metres, longwave radio signals (submarine communications via the ionosphere-bouncing devices like HAARP/SURA/JUNO, etc.) at around 10^4 metres and more, or a wavelength of between 4-9 kilometres, the TV and FM radio operates on a wavelength of a metre or so.

Incidentally, we have absolutely no idea how these commonly used frequencies affect humans. The mind boggles when one considers what might happen to other dimensional entities in the eventuality that they operate in a magnetic environment, for that is where the effects are implemented.

This may sound mysterious but it is straightforward science, however, we don't see, feel or taste any of this, and indeed it is mysterious for the individual who limits themselves to a worldview of pure physicality, restricted by the interaction between our sense organs and the phenomenal world.

Regrettably, and this of course expresses my belief alone, so no aspersions on the faith and convictions of others, I have yet to find a religion that makes a satisfactory (i.e. logical) explanation of all this. There is only one philosophy in the extant history of man that provides a coherent story as to how the whole ticks, so Vedanta forms the basis for my understanding and explanation here.

We humans systematically have at some stage, if not throughout the totality of our physical existence, a conviction that we are nothing more than a physical entity, and I daresay that we lose the idea of being anything but. We are informed that even though we are a mass of bacteria with a very large majority of space in between each molecule, we are humans with various capacities – mainly the one to work and a duty to stay busy. Our focus is elsewhere than the potential nature of our true Self.

It is hard to find the time to sit and contemplate the nature of life, and there is no encouragement even to do so – we've got it all covered for you; we being the temporal authorities of education, government and (so-called) healthcare.

Where can there possibly be space for a Self in this pressure cooker world that we appear to be surviving in?

Even less, where is there space for any concern for things we do not normally see?

Having said that, so many factors involved in the maintenance of the human organism point to a totally neglected aspect of physiology, and those same principles are intensely involved in the day-to-day operation of the world. Whilst these factors are equally ignored or poorly explained, they become easier to appreciate and more logical when considered from the angle of magnetism.

I personally believe that the domain of magnetism holds universes of potential which we are either not equipped, or more likely, simply do not bother to investigate. The reason for this conviction is that there is an intriguing and systematic feature of the human magnetic spectrum.

It would be impossible to prove because to my knowledge there is no magnetometer sensitive enough to measure the human magnetic charge, but when someone dies, we know that the electric current, as shown on the ECG drops to zero, but the magnetic reading of a dead human <u>systematically</u>, when using a pendulum and chart reveals a measurement of 15, no more nor less. Quite what this implies is full of interest to my mind, for there can be no doubt that there is some form of existence present – of a very different nature from the type of existence that we know and experience in this human life form.

There would seem to be a case to be argued that this magnetic link is related to what we might term the spirit connection. We live in a magnetic environment on the earth, we are magnetic creatures – with a stronger field of force when alive because of the flows of vital energy, blood, nerve and meridian.

This can be readily discovered using a pendulum and a chart with a scale of 0 to 120, as shown in the Analysis Method chapter below. One simply asks, "What is the magnetic or biomagnetic reading of this person?" It ranges in measurement from 15 to 75 and will be found to be an immensely useful indicator of human well-being; there is no unit of measurement *per se* and no registering of the electron spin or other movement. The unit of measurement used to record the magnetic field of the earth is a microtesla, ranging between 25 and 65 microteslas for the earth's charge, I suspect that this same value can be applied to a human reading. Quite what this expression of movement is can be explained in a variety of ways, but I don't think that really helps our understanding. It is probably a function of the life energy, the Chinese *qi* or the Vedic *prana*. The strength of such an element in a living human varies according to many factors: exposure to electromagnetic radiation, the strength or otherwise of the immune system, the wearing of shoes, environmental influences, physical sickness, emotional well-being, and so on.

Whilst alive this magnetic charge can be boosted, and that is very good news because our entire environment is gradually being weakened magnetically as a result of the use of electricity, mobile telephony, pollution of all sorts and radiation, etc..

What could be more natural than for other forms of unknown, and unknowable, life exist in the environment we inhabit. When you learn that even the insects use more of the electromagnetic spectrum (infrared especially) than us humans, you begin to get an idea of our limited capacity in that area. What is more, we can only presume the dimensions in which the insects exist, explaining it as a function of our more limited human experience.

Taking this analogy to the life-death cycle, we can start to appreciate that we are really in the dark, unless we work from the angle of frequency, and that could well form a very useful, albeit tentative basis

OTHER-DIMENSIONAL ENTITIES

from which to start any investigation.

It would be arrogant and vain to claim any understanding as to how or where these entities or domains actually exist or function, but the evidence in literature, cultural traditions, personal experience all point to a definite kind of reality in their respect. You know when you have had a run-in with a ghost or ghoul!

Furthermore, it does not matter how to prove anything in this respect, because proof is not available. Proof is a scientific requirement, subject to all sorts of rigorous conditions, which are neither relevant nor possible in the spaces we are talking about. The counter-argument to refute that is unfortunately unavailable too. So, we are cast onto the unreliable for some, authentic for others, intuition which we all seem to share – to a certain degree, and that degree is not very scientifically calibrated either.

There is, however, a very real misconception as regards life, as in birth and death; these last two are occurrences confined to the waking state alone. The 'world' is a manifestation of life in the waking state alone, because it is not present in deep sleep, nor in the dream state, so the world can not be a creation of the mind, as some would have us believe, but that is such a vast subject and not quite the topic here.

If one is able to consider what we intuit or know within ourselves, namely existence, without any need for material proof, because that is not pertinent in any other domain except the material – and can recognize that this state of 'being' is to be found in every state we experience as humans, even are fundamentally, then one is not far from accessing the notion of "spirit", which is the basis of all that we experience, and then some.

It takes little imagination to conceive of the suffering felt by a dead person, on losing their physical envelope, when the earthly waking existence comes to an end. That will be made even worse as a result of attachment to body, family, property or other, when they find themselves in limbo, so to speak. Who is there to help? Is help even a possibility?

Answers to such questions can only be accepted if the methods proposed have achieved the necessary personal objective as a result of extensive and repetitive experience. None of those methods, to my understanding, can be initially based on logic or reasoning. Intuition is key. Therefore, confidence, not only in your own conviction, but your intimate gnosis is essential, otherwise doubt and cerebral influences move in, take over and let's go and have another beer.

To complicate matters, we do not possess an adequate vocabulary to express notions beyond the physical; secondly, the language we do employ tends to be highly object-oriented, coloured by education and agenda; thirdly, when we are talking of this other dimensional entity phenomenon, we are in a sphere where words perhaps no longer hold currency. We are beyond symbolism, we are in existence itself, in Life in another form than the kinetic, but Life nevertheless.

Our ability to connect our physical, spiritual and mental realities seamlessly with all that exists is key. Spirit readily communicates with spirit.

This latter statement is one of the most important to my mind when dealing with medical, psychic, and psychological affairs. This is how we should relate to each other and everything around us, even though we are unlikely to put it in so many words.

My apprehension of sensationalism, especially of a new-age variety associated with certain words, causes me to steer clear of what some call "angels" or "guides." Even though their characteristics probably merit such names, these anonymous presences, who demonstrate the most remarkable patience and extraordinary kindness as they seemingly show us the way around, and even out of the restricted recognition most of us believe to be reality, correspond more to the *hun* (more on them at the end of the book) and are probably nothing more nor less than a spark of the Superior Intelligence, or God if you prefer.

It makes me chuckle when I hear that we humans, in the western world at least, are civilised. For those of you who have spent time in other 'civilisations', you may well appreciate the irony of that when one considers the way people in other more 'primitive' cultures treat their dying. While we in the west may have criteria that must be reached and maintained in modern society if we wish to claim membership of such an illustrious group, it seems reasonable that this same standard is, or should be, applied across the board. That is not the case, however, because from a materialistic standpoint, life and death become a personal matter, for each to sort out according to his/her own understanding. That is probably the natural consequence of assuming the physical component of the human to be the end of the story. We all know, or at least suspect, that is not the case, but there is so much emphasis put on the material aspects of the physical experience that it is understandably hard to come to terms with the alternative view of being essentially a spiritual medium, let alone accept that we are part of a spiritual whole.

One of the sequels of a materialistic approach to life appears to be a loss of the values of concern for the other, not because it brings you merit or brownie points to be kind to others – I don't know, but because if the idea of spirit connection is real, you ARE the other.

CHAPTER 4
OTHER DIMENSIONAL ENTITY MANIFESTATION

Sensation, gross or subtle, is perhaps the first indication that one is in the company of an entity, or entities. In that context, you might well imagine that the most upsetting for our everyday human sensitivity is when the presence is accompanied by smell. I would defy anyone to define the origin of the odour; at best, one can recognize putrescence and the breakdown of organic matter, but it somehow defies the mind's capacity to nail how something so banal as a smell can, all at the same time, be threatening, evil and sickening beyond belief.

Fortunately, such malodorous incidents are rare, but definitely a warning that you are in the presence of what one can easily describe as pure evil. Far more frequent are the gross manifestations specific to the other three Aristotelian senses – taste seems to be spared, but sight and sound are the most common means for other dimensional entities to express their presence, touch is not unusual and borders on smell with regard to the fear factor, but more on that later. While sighting is the probably the most common way for other dimensional entities to appear, sound comes in a close second, we have all heard of poltergeists throwing things around or making plenty of noise, as if determined to

OTHER-DIMENSIONAL ENTITIES

make you aware of their discomfort or displeasure, but subtle noises are very often an indication of other dimensional entities.

Is the evidence of their existence somehow related to their former physical expression? I don't know and although that might be of importance in some way or another, the fact remains that they have demonstrated that they are here. It would be easy enough to state that they are in the wrong dimension for their current state, but what better way to draw attention to that situation, and perhaps even find someone who can release them. Of course, that is my anthropocentric way of looking at the picture, and staking a claim to the benefit of what I spend much of my time doing.

There are probably many ways in which an other dimensional entity might make itself visible, or at least present, but generally they seem to be subtle – like a breath of air on your skin of a calm, windless day. In all likelihood, it is only if you are in a position to do something to help the other dimensional entity on its way, that you will be solicited. There is no doubt that there are what is known in the 'trade' as jokers and tricksters, whoever has tried the Ouija board or the three-legged table to contact 'spirits' will have encountered such phenomena, it is fortunately easy enough with the simple 'thumbkey' hand mudra, to know whether one is dealing with an authentic other dimensional entity, or not. That will be explored further on.

It is one more example on my part when I express the possible method as to how other dimensional entities operate of my very limited understanding, governed by my human condition, but the fact remains, one has to start from that position of sensual and intellectual boundary if one hopes to achieve any kind of progress, so please bear with me, adding your input so as to reach a clearer picture.

Next to visual sighting of other dimensional entities, a very frequently reported phenomenon is physical contact. How often have I been called upon to help figure out what can only be termed 'freak accidents'?

A man of 60 years of age bicycling along a road in Taipei was suddenly pushed from behind and projected into the road, cracking his skull, breaking a few bits and pieces, before his niece contacts me to ask if I can cast a little light on to the situation. Sure enough, or so it seemed, he had been pushed by some force that wanted to hurt him – and it succeeded. The long and the short of it all was that there was a seedy tale involving money and an unpaid debt. That force was very much

Chapter 4

in control of the injured man, who recovered consciousness a week or so later, but was not to release its hold while I was involved. There are some cases where one learns that it is best not to get involved, and the considerable time spent on questioning and sharing the findings were never offset.

Early one morning in Chiang Mai, our housekeeper called me urgently to patch up her son who had driven off the road on his motorbike on his way to school. Nothing life-threatening, but some nasty scratches, and the firm conviction that he was unable to turn the handlebars to negotiate the curve in the road.

Sure enough, there was this spot, well-known in the neighbourhood for its unhealthy reputation, with sightings of dog-like creatures and what I can only attribute to Thai folklore. The energy levels on my chart was pretty horrible, with spirit presence around the old wooden house thirty or so metres in from the road, I cleared that and returned to the road, which now appeared to be a normal thoroughfare, the black *sha* – as our *feng shui* friends would have it, having been removed. The lad recovered but was always a little wary when taking that curve.

Much closer to the bone, and the most singular sensation of touch is what one could term "grasping hands". An alarming experience to be grabbed by the ankle as you are climbing the stairs, in such a manner that you are unable to move up or down. Once the clearing was made, the "hands" stopped their antics. Quite what was the cause has rarely been the subject of my questioning, there is an urgency to relieve the other dimensional entity, and the rest is relatively academic.

The history of Northern Thailand (Lanna – the million rice-fields) is ancient and closely entwined with that of the Shan state in neighbouring Burma. I built my house next to a spa resort to the north of the city, the foolhardiness of the spa owners soon became apparent, because they had built it on an old burial ground, and it was full of active other dimensional entities, including some aggressive Burmese soldiers who had their own way of drawing attention to their plight. One day playing tennis with the spa manager, as was our wont, I was thrown violently to the ground, shaken and bruised I got to my feet only to be called urgently by a receptionist to come and fetch my youngest son who had just broken his arm falling off one of the exercise machines, four hundred yards away. Off to the hospital to have the boy's arm checked and plastered, before returning to the spa to thank the receptionist and clear the decks of the four or five senior officers who had been there for

OTHER-DIMENSIONAL ENTITIES

three hundred years or so, suggesting that their colleagues would only have to ask in the future if I could be of service.

I had not tripped, the court surface was perfectly dry and uniform, but I had felt that my legs were swept from beneath me, and my tennis partner was taken aback by the whole performance although I did not risk my version of the story in view of his active scepticism to such matters.

Some of the more unpleasant accounts of hauntings involve the other dimensional entity apparently oppressing their victim, sitting on their chest and suffocating them. It is a very real and painful experience, often with associated trauma close by. The other dimensional entity's suffering at the time of their death seems to be repeated in the encounter with the victim as a very physical and frequently, violent sensation.

CHAPTER 5
ALTERNATIVE RELEASE PROCESSES

Probably the first obstacle one encounters when dealing with the subject of other dimensional entity or spirit release is how to get the message across to one's interlocutor; using language they are able to understand without alarming or scaring them, or even worse, giving them the impression that you, or they should be tied up in a straightjacket! A serious minefield, where intuition plays its hand, but by carefully listening to the other person one probably finds the right form of compassionate understanding, allowing subsequent meaningful communication.

Fortunately, there is an increasing awareness of the anomaly caused by entity presence. It has so many and diverse ways of appearing and they cannot all be put down to a fertile imagination, or the hackneyed favourite "It's all in your head, go see the shrink." Despite the best will in the world, and there are surely a great many doctors, therapists and carers who are concerned and would fervently like to help, but their hands are tied by the modern medical paradigm, in addition to a singular scarcity of those who might be able to provide a solution.

That is hardly surprising if we are not even able to determine exactly what constitutes death. If there is doubt about the cessation of activity in the physical envelope, what hope can we expect from that quarter concerning any other possible form of existence, let alone any form of interaction with it.

Who does one approach to deal with these issues? There are not many signboards in the street out there for people who might be capable of dealing with the problem. While it is definitely a task for some kind of specialist, there is no recognised protocol, training or method. It would perhaps be unwise to say that there is one method that works, let alone one person who is competent and another not. It is a very subjective affair, as I said above there is no instruction manual, particularly in this domain. If a clearing works for someone and the passage of time proves the release is efficient and the individual's life assumes 'normality', what can one say, and where is there a need for anything to be said?

Nevertheless, there seem to be few who are able to work a 'cure'. And when the word cure is used, it should be understood as permanent, without relapse or incident unless brought on by the individual's own habit, infelicity or lack of attention.

The first and most important question to ask the person proposing help would, in my mind, be "Where do you send them?" Depending on the answer, one takes a decision to work with them or not.

You have no doubt noticed that all accounts of near death experience (NDE) mention a tunnel and light. There are some rather sophisticated scientific theories as to how that happens and it would be expressing one more vain opinion to elaborate further on that, but it is a notable common denominator which corresponds to the fundamental nature of what we experience as Consciousness.

What we do have as a shared and totally common experience in life for us humans, is the light.

That light, whether we recognize it or not, is present in waking, dream and deep sleep, because without it there would be no notion of continuity of life. So by force of its existence as we experience it, and by logical inference, it can be viewed as a constant to all known forms of life that we know. Consequently, it is both the source, inasmuch as we are able to conceive of such, and by inference, the destination also.

Light is a rather weak term for this ever-present being that hangs out wherever we are, at all times and in all situations. Its apparent absence in deep sleep is negated when on waking you are asked if you slept well, and reply, 'like a log' or some such. There must have been something there to have witnessed your being – therefore with no second to observe the first. So, from here on, that light will be referred to as the light of Self, or simply Self to differentiate it from the light bulb.

So, it might be a good idea to understand the therapist's notion of the 'right place' for the human spirit once the physical envelope has been shed.

The benefit of a disembodied entity reaching the light, is that a return to this dimension of human existence is then impossible, without assuming another material envelope. While that statement is open to debate, there is a certain logic to it. I would not expect anyone to accept what I say as the truth, until they have put it to the test for themselves, but what I say here has been confirmed by beings I believe to be reliable sources.

Anywhere else than the origin and finality of existence could be considered as limbo, a no-man's-land dimension with no known parameters for guidance or limitation. Not exactly the place one could wish for, nevertheless a distinct possibility in much the same way that the infra-red diapason of frequency enables the insect universe to operate, yet we are unable to sense those frequencies.

A vital condition for the continuity of a harmonious and decent form of natural existence is the avoidance of hurting each other. I would include consideration and care for other dimensional entities in that context. Obviously, if our so-called education does not address that aspect, there develops a domain where no control, no moral compass is applied, and the potential for damage and harm is limitless. I would venture that there is perhaps a connection with that state of lawlessness and modern society?

The Roman Catholic approach

What I find particularly alarming with the exorcism process of the Catholic church is that the sole purpose is the casting out of a demonic entity. It is not a matter of ensuring a passage to a better space, just removal of the nasty thing; it is definitely not a comprehensive approach to any kind of improvement for the unfortunate victim, the invading entity or entities, the society concerned, nor for future implications. It is a conflict between good (the church) and evil (Satan). There is no room for any nuance between black and white, and even less for compassion.

OTHER-DIMENSIONAL ENTITIES

I find it very hard to believe that the Christ's casting out of legion as recounted on several occasions in the New Testament in the Bible was limited to such a base act as to despatch the other dimensional entities into a herd of pigs, who then ran off a cliff to their deaths. Either this shows only respect for human life and too bad for the pigs, or the notion of empathy needs some serious revision.

Gabriele Amorth, may he rest in peace, was the Vatican exorcist for many years. He reputedly worked on multiple occasions on the same person to remove the <u>same</u> demonic entity. That cannot reasonably be considered as a clearing, it is a fight, with return performances to show who is the strongest. In my book, that is neither efficient, nor merciful, and definitely not beneficial.

It is scarcely surprising then that Amorth stated that Satan is in the Vatican. One can infer from this that some form of serious competition is being played out. Whatever the outcome, and wherever exorcism occurs, the purpose is <u>not</u> relief for those involved, it would appear to be a vulgar power struggle, as if in some kind of political arena, and as a result, one can reach the distasteful conclusion that the church is losing having lost the focus on human welfare.

There is no doubt that in the cases involving satanism and black magic, one is dealing with evil, pure, manifest destruction whose sole aim is to hurt whilst striving for their objective. Fortunately it is not encountered every time one approaches a case, but the practitioner is well advised to not only know of this contingency, but to be forearmed and prepared – either to steer clear or to find the suitable approach.

The actual method used to remove an entity in the Catholic exorcism process involves formula and prayer. I.e. words, or frequencies from a certain viewpoint. We are totally unaware as to how these frequencies actually function, let alone the method of communication between a 'living' person and a disembodied entity. What authority do those formula hold to make the other dimensional entity move on? It is not surprising then that the same entity has to be addressed on numerous occasions. That method does not always work and Amorth admitted it. We are not told where the destination of the other dimensional entity is geographically, nor the conditions existing there, it could even be a repository for future recruits of black magicians, if Satan is in the Vatican as Amorth said!

Whilst on the topic of religion, there is a strong argument which could well find its place when giving thanatological advice. If I understand correctly, the Roman Catholic faith states that adherents must wait for the second coming before redemption and eternal life is ensured. Such dogma could well lead to confusion in the minds of the faithful, do we take the tunnel now, or should we wait for the man? There seems to be no incompatibility to waiting in the light, rather than holding on in the so-called dimension of the living, but if that debate is going on in your head, indecision is guaranteed. A word of encouragement to opt for the light to the dying person might be advisable.

Hypno-therapy approach

This is probably the best known and most commonly practised method of spirit release. Ever since Carl Wickland wrote his book, *Thirty Years Among the Dead* in 1924, hypnosis seems to be the preferred method. I could and would not debate the validity as I have never tried it, it seems to work as so many authors have since sung its praise.

What I do know, however, is that it requires the physical presence of the patient, someone able to hypnotise, and often that of a channeler too. Limiting those involved strikes me as being a singular advantage. There is an argument for numbers adding weight to encouraging the entity to leave, but most of the time the latter are ready for that. From a purely practical viewpoint, any unnecessary exposure to potentially hostile entities is best dealt with by restricting the participants to the practitioner and the patient.

Once again, this approach is performed thanks to the use of words, in the language of the hypnotist, word-frequencies which we assume are received and acted upon by the entity. It is a pretty shaky argument in my reckoning, but if that works, so much the better. I for one am not convinced.

What is more intriguing to my mind is the fact that the words of reassurance and convincing argument are sufficient to change the mind of the entity to renounce their current space and head off to some destination recommended by a (generally) complete stranger. For that is what Louise Ireland-Frey suggests in her book, *Freeing the Captives*, and so much the better if it works. It does, however, raise a number of questions:

1/ Is there sufficient authority in the words of a human, unknown in all probability to the entity, to make them change their 'thinking', and accept the proferred release?

2/ Is not such a method solely dependent on the practitioner's intention? (there is no doubt that intention is the very basis of the whole idea of spirit release, one wants to help any way possible, but...)

3/ [The most uncomfortable question] Are we (practitioners) not perhaps deluding ourselves, thinking that we are able to interfere in the spirit world using means that are specific to the material world? Namely, logical reasoning, rather than empathetic conviction, or that dreadfully vague word, intention, or whatever it is.

These are more than rhetorical questions, and although it is unlikely that complete answers will be forthcoming to the general satisfaction, they are valid and well worth contemplating if you want to find a sure-fire method of achieving the objective of helping the other dimensional entity and bringing relief to the victim.

As in so many domains of activity today, there are those who make phenomenal claims – generally with a price tag in keeping, counting on and profiting from the gullibility and desperation of those involved. Take your pendulum and ask what colour are they, would be my recommendation and choice means. If you are in serious doubt, check with a competent kinesiological or arm-muscle test method. It is not possible to furnish proof to the satisfaction of one and all of entity presence or absence, in the same way, a clearing cannot be substantiated.

Having sown a serious doubt in your minds, it might be best to leave this for the time being and move on to the essential topic of possession.

CHAPTER 6
PLAIN VANILLA POSSESSION AND COMMON OR GARDEN OBSESSION

Possession is a rather alarming word, but for lack of a better expression it does conjure up the desired image of a person not being alone in their own integrity, and perhaps even influenced by some form of external or foreign energy. Try not to read too much into the word, focus more on the influence that energy works.

In my fifteen years' experience of collecting statistics, there seems to be an average of 65% of the public who are affected by this phenomenon of 'possession'.

From among that 65% of the population with other dimensional entities, there seems to be a larger proportion with just one attachment. The maximum number I have found attached to one person was nineteen; that appeared to be due to multiple stays in hospital. He was a young lad of fourteen, and the only apparent manifestation of the infestation was clumsiness. When offered the chance of clearing, they were apparently all happy to head out of town to the light. The adolescent concerned had not even formulated in his mind that there was anything amiss, it was all part of his 'world'.

There are no rules in this domain, one entity and you can have schizophrenia, nineteen and a clumsy lad. The Catholic exorcist would not even dream of working on such a case, there is no evidence of satanic presence.

Whilst on the subject of schizophrenia, it is hard to witness in such cases that no change occurs for the host when the entity(ies) do leave, for the simple reason most of the time medication has taken its heavy toll, and for the host it is as if nothing has happened despite the invading entity no longer being present. The problem is that this medical condition takes time to develop before it is defined as such, and there are few, if any, doctors who would risk their reputation and career by calling on the kind of help discussed here.

It might be useful to mention some of the signs that indicate uninvited and unwanted entity presence. Once again there are no rules, standards or stages, and the following might even be due to nutritional tendencies, but are, nevertheless, often found in instances of possession:

- Hearing internal voices
- Recurring mental messages
- Involuntary actions
- Addictions
- Obsessional behaviour
- Abnormal behaviour
- Untoward medical conditions.

The reasons for possession, as if there is such a thing as cause and effect in the spirit world (!), are many, with new ones possibly being found every day. There do, however, seem to be certain conditions, common to all lands and cultures. Those reasons can be divided into two sub-categories: Voluntary and involuntary, with the latter probably being the most common of the two.

Involuntary possession

Generally, the problem follows a loss of consciousness due to anaesthesia, epilepsy, fainting, inebriation, being stoned,... The individual in such a condition is unaware of their exposure, therefore defenceless and open to invasion. Invasion of their vital space, that zone of the human psyche where no one ventures to clarify what might be going on, let alone how, and the complexity is confounded by the inability of the average doctor, despite their possible goodwill, suggesting that the psychiatrist needs to be consulted. Our lack of education regarding possibilities of other dimensional beings is exemplary, and desperately damaging. Once again, for those interested, I have added an appendix to share my understanding of this quintessential aspect.

Nevertheless, when in that space of oblivion, the person has no awareness of their environment, devoid of their intuitive and mental capacities which might normally protect them, and the entity has free access to their "space", and due to lack of prior instruction and outright egocentricity, will muscle in.

Depending on the determination, perhaps the strength of character/personality of the invading entity, what happens next is a new life for the subject. There may be no change, or there may be war. This is why people who do reach out for help are open to the idea that 'something is not right', those unaware and not bothered by the invader will not react so docilely to a suggestion that they have a hanger-on!

Stress, death of close ones, hanging out in areas or with people of low energy (negativity), are also some of the factors leading to possession. There are no standards here, there is just the amazing universe of desperation.

Voluntary possession

What could be more natural on the loss of a comrade on a battlefield? Or seeing a close friend drowning, and when pulling them from the water, you agree to them sharing your vital space? A close relative to whom you are strongly attached, how can you refuse their final appeal?

You begin to grasp the complexity and the subtlety of the possibilities.

The categories of an involuntary nature are equally diverse, but range much further to include the complex diapason of curse which we will cover later.

Piggy-back

This is a commonly encountered situation when one finds several other dimensional entities in the individual, and questioning reveals that one or more of them have or had no personal relationship with the client. Bear in mind that the invading entity might have made 'friends' between the time of losing their physical envelope and the time of moving into their new home. Such errant souls are common and are generally quite shy, not responding to questioning, and often lacking in human reaction. By careful questioning, always seek them out, and if there, send them to the light.

Shy other dimensional entities

Of a similar nature to above, but avoiding contact if at all possible with humans for whatever reason. Sometimes associated with black magic, as such an entity does not want to be revealed, so they can continue working their mischief, or simply because they are not complete. I have seen the term 'fragments' used in texts on spirits, and I would be inclined to place that category in this context. There is no point trying to force information from an entity who may have lost their memory, limbs, whatever, it is not our role to resolve entity trauma, it is our job to help them to the light.

Low energy locations

In the same way that there are high energy areas ('hot spots'), natural or man-made, it would seem normal that the equivalent, at the opposite end of the scale, also exist. It might be the work of the imagination, but I would put my scepticism to one side, and accept that places where humans have undergone suffering, areas of repetitive lightning strike, burial grounds, strong adverse telluric (geological) influences, and similar, can act as host to a gathering of entities, either because humans do not choose to congregate there, or because they feel more comfortable in such zones. Almost invariably in my dowsing work in such zones, spirit presence is associated with low energetic readings from telluric sources.

Addiction

This physical dimension of ours appears to be highly addictive. We form a strong attachment to so many aspects of our life without having any idea at all as to what is really happening, but we hang on in grim desperation even when we are hurting, and others are wondering why we don't just let go and die.

I would propose here that addiction can also be more than the human propensity for pleasure, and the ignorance of where that really lies. There is good cause to believe that entities might have a hand in this area of human suffering. There is no education worth the name that encourages us to avoid addiction. Yet we all shun anyone tarnished with that condition, and feel sorry for them. It is a question of degree, we are all addicted otherwise, we would not be in human form.

The other dimensional entities of addiction must be what keep the world fixated in human awareness. It is a mere blur between attachment and addiction; a blur that bites and burrows until the whole collapses into absorption in the physical. Only the awareness of that, in other words, a firm "STOP!" can bring the other dimensional entity-wagon to a halt. Not until the individual is strong enough to apply the necessary force to restore harmony, can it be achieved. Till that time addiction, or external entities oblige the person to keep the habit. What is problematic in such cases is that no matter how often the entities are released from an addict, there will always be others happy to replace the predecessors.

There is a convincing argument for reincarnation when one reflects on one's addiction to 'life'.

The removal/release of entities from someone plagued by addiction can only be cosmetic, like applying a new layer of makeup, it is done to please those loving and caring souls suffering from the agony of the addict, those obliged to watch the descent.

Of course, there is an advantage to releasing the entities who ensure addiction, obsession, compulsion and damaging habits, that avoids them returning to new hosts, this limiting the damage that results, and hopefully showing them a little compassion as they move on their way. It is a good idea, as always in such cases, but maybe more so, to ask if the entities are in agreement.

As a therapist performing entity-release work, I do not think I have an educational role, even if such is possible. The emphasis must be on harmony, and providing release.

In the Process chapter above we have looked at a possible cause for the origination of an other dimensional entity, namely their opting for the familiar physical dimension, and refusing the beckoning light. We can now move onto even thinner ice, how and where do they move around, and I believe, gather together?

OTHER-DIMENSIONAL ENTITIES

CHAPTER 7
SOLITUDE OR COMMUNAL LIVING

It is easy to imagine the frustration felt by a former human when they can no longer communicate and be recognized as a human as of the time they have no more physical envelope. That frustration could well be turned into a more aggressive approach, as in 'let's take over another envelope!' And where are those to be found? Assuming that the other dimensional entity in its new status can figure this out, the primary source would logically be a hospital, as mentioned earlier. People not only lose their lives there in a higher ratio than any other establishment, but there are lots of inanimate, comatose or drugged bodies lying around.

The options for our errant entity, recently deprived of a physical body, and looking for a new 'home', seem to be two: move into another human and see how things pan out, or resign to being a solitary entity.

If my figures are correct of the number of people who are host to other dimensional entities is 65% of the population, that means a lot of disembodied entities on the loose who have refused the light.

A normal human tendency is to form communal groups, so it could be a reasonable assumption that the solitary entity does, or tries to do, the same thing. In the course of my work around the world, I have found that entities tend to group together in areas which the living shun. Nowhere in my experience, however, has the density of such entities been found to be so intense as in Ireland. Perhaps that is because Ireland is so sparsely populated? I think not, nor is it because the living shun the Emerald Isle.

This manifests in a rather startling way. Whereas the numbers of entities would be found in the tens, possibly scores in Southeast Asia and the Far East, continental Europe and the USA. In Ireland, they are generally in the thousands, frequently in the 5-7 range. The possible causes remain academic unless someone is prepared for some serious offbeat, historical research.

After several years of encountering these surprisingly high numbers, logic and intuition would indicate that the history of the country, with its imposed foreign – in all senses of the word – beliefs and mores, might well be at the root of the phenomenon. The original or early beliefs of the people have been crushed, whether it was Druidism or a form of Irish Christianity, and they have resigned – in some confusion I would venture – to the idea of having to wait for the second coming in order to access paradise. The intense spiritual suffering that has caused makes for a special mentality, which is indeed found expressed in the kindness, tolerance and gaiety of the people.

However that may be and forgive me for going off on a tangent, the solution, or what I can only hope to be such, for the relief of these myriad souls is to ask the traditional questions of the entities and send those who are ready to move to the light on their way. I mention this because it might well be a good way of providing some solace, not only to the entities but to all those in the neighbourhood.

What I am about to say concerning travel by the entities amounts to speculation, I have never had it confirmed by a friendly entity, but I have obtained the answers using a pendulum. They are able to change location, although they generally stay close to where they recently lived; if they do travel, they can use waterways, which is why they are generally to be found in low-lying areas where water flows, and also why possession often takes place when the person is in telluric contact with underground water especially.

Despite the damage done by communism, autocratic regimes and materialism, throughout China, Southeast Asia and the Far East special attention is given to entities, by and large they are venerated, acknowledged and cared for, although probably not particularly liked. The same applies to Islamic countries, there is a respect and special place given to the *ruh*. Would it be an exaggeration to suggest that as a result, their presence is limited compared to those countries where Christianity is practised. Our western religions and belief systems are simply not oriented towards care for the disembodied.

Whilst on that subject, a word might be usefully said concerning organ transplants. There is a very strong chance that the impressions, desires and tendencies carry over from the donor to the organ receiver. It can be quite alarming for the receiver to experience such 'emotions', and the medical profession could well pay more careful attention to this, but there is little chance that such superstition will be attended to. It is one more aspect for the therapist to be aware of. It does seem possible to help such people, but a lot of conviction is often required before they will allow you access.

Some years ago at a psychic and holistic fair in County Cork, a young man started a conversation with me after reading the blurb on the table regarding the services I offer. The long and short of it led to my clearing an other dimensional entity, and more out of concern than curiosity, I asked him if he would like to talk about it. He had received the lungs of a young man killed in a motor bike accident, as his own organs were severely compromised and his days were numbered without a transplant. He categorically refused to elaborate on the nature of the problem that he was now confronted with, but it was obviously one of considerable scope and only his immediate family were in the know. My pendulum indicated that it was an issue with one of the *po*, normal enough, they reside in the lungs, but he was not to be drawn. Some three years later he stopped at my stand at Skibbereen farmers' market with his girl-friend to say hello. When I asked how the lungs were doing, he smiled and replied that he was much better, and things were grand.

One can only imagine the frame of mind (heart) for the receiver of a pig's heart. I no longer have a pig or pigs, but at one stage in Thailand my farm was host to 63 of them, in France there had always been two or so on the homestead. I mention this because I don't think I have ever encountered an animal so able to communicate, and that applies to boar, white and pot-belly varieties. It is the first time I have ever expressed this, as it strikes me as being remarkable faculty; I would venture they think it is par for the course!

The same applies to the transfusion of blood, it is definitely worth checking whether the person's colour has changed to violet (other dimensional entity presence) after the transfusion, and then performing a clearance. That recently happened to a friend who had been in hospital with an immune system problem and had received several transfusions. The liver is the organ where blood is stored in the body, and of course the seat of the *hun*. Whose *hun* is the question. This adds yet another intriguing element to the whole affair, and would seem to indicate that we are made up of all sorts of bits and pieces, some with unsuspected capacities.

Part of the assessment in the method I use when diagnosing a person is to ask how many *hun* and *po* are present in the person under study.

In the course of the last year, many people have been injected with unknown substances reputedly to protect them against some ill-defined condition. The side-effects of this injection, let alone the boosters, are numerous and increasing; that is a medically recognized fact. Given that we have no symptomology for affairs of the spirit, it is of considerable interest when working on the principles of Traditional Chinese Medicine (TCM) to learn that of all the people who have been injected there is a possible discrepancy in the numbers, at least among those whom I have diagnosed. Almost systematically, the number of *hun* is down to two, instead of three; the *po* numbers fluctuate, from 4 to 5 out of 7.

In all cases where people who have shared their intimate details as regards changes that have occurred since the injection, there is a common complaint, "things are not the same". The symptoms range from total loss of dowsing capacity, facial neuropathy, deficient kidney function, breathing issues, brain fog, difficulty in maintaining mental focus, a sense of alienation from others, greater than "normal" emotional imbalance, and often a combination of these. All these people have a strong sense that something is very wrong within themselves, and there is considerable motivation to find a solution.

Where to start? Is it possible to bring the missing *hun* and *po* back? From the TCM standpoint, the Du Mai or Governor Vessel would be a logical place to start, the Du 4 (Gate of Vitality) point could well be a useful one to treat the kidneys, as it reinforces the *yang* of the kidneys, and especially to work on the essences and the spirits (*shen*). Du 14 might also be a useful point, as it calms the *shen* while stimulating *yang*. There is every benefit from working on various Urinary Bladder points on the back, BL 42. *Po Hu*, the gate of the *Po*; BL 43, *Gao Huang*, where the demons can hide between the heart and the diaphragm, often associated with shallow breathing; BL 44, *Shen Tang*, the hall of the *shen*; BL 47, *Hun Men*, the door of the *Hun*.

Nature is so merciful and works in ways so far beyond human imagination, however this time round we have perhaps overstepped the limit, and may well have no other option but to help ourselves out of the pickle we are in. Clearly there is not enough feedback to make any claims with regard to useful solutions, but often the pendulum indicates colloidal electrum (gold and silver) as being a useful therapy, as it decalcifies the pineal gland amongst other benefits. Gold is an energy booster as well as a hormonal balancer, silver, of course, is anti-viral, anti-inflammatory and anti-bacterial.

A homeopathic preparation of the various vaccines is surely an avenue to explore, as suggested recently by a homeopath friend, but it seems unlikely that would be sufficient to recover the *hun* or *po* who have posted absent.

As mentioned elsewhere, much of my work involves trying to repair the damage caused by malevolent individuals, whether using entities to do their bidding or not, and that seems to be the next topic to investigate.

OTHER-DIMENSIONAL ENTITIES

CHAPTER 8
BLACK MAGIC

Exchanges with knowledgeable people, reading, often between the lines, and fifty-odd years of experience in these unexplored regions we are discussing, have led me to a certain number of practical conclusions concerning the practice of magic, especially black magic. In the interest of avoiding sensationalism, to which I would add I am totally allergic, this sordid subject needs to be addressed, and a clear position in this respect needs to be assumed in the mind of the practitioner.

At some stage in the practice of black magic, there arises the opportunity – generally needs-based, to acquire help. The magician finds their activity to be limited, and the only solution is to recruit assistance to perform the tasks that only a disembodied entity is able to do. Another human is of course an option, but the effort and disadvantages involved soon eliminate that option. Remember that these types of people (the magician) are not generally operating alone, nor are they working solely for their own interests, they are available for hire, often in covens, for the benefit of their abject master.

In the very probable contingency that other dimensional entities are everywhere, but they do seem to have a tendency to congregate in low energy zones (geopathic stress, waterways – the latter can be used as transport, areas of stagnation, abandoned regions), hospitals and places where people lose their lives. It seems reasonable to assume that burial grounds are probably a rich recruiting zone for competent black magicians. We are all prone to the allure of a smile, after all communication is a human necessity, and while that can assume several forms, they are all based on affinity or love. Acknowledgement of presence – bodily or otherwise – is the first step, closely followed by acquiring the subject's name. Remember the first thing Christ asks on meeting the troubled person was the name of the invading entity.

Having been introduced, so to speak, the ground is open for the magician to seduce and inveigle the subject. What happens then is not our business, even though we are obliged to help restore what we can of the original love and harmony, and the latter are the only way to proceed.

Although examples of individual experience may be of use, I personally find them redundant and with a whiff of sensationalism, so I will recount only such experiences as provide an example of what might well be used, learned from - even followed, by the potential practitioner.

The encounter with the tool of the magician, for that is what such an entity becomes, is best kept to a minimum for obvious reasons of contamination, seduction and corruption. Arm's length would be the best advice.

I recount this story because it tells of how I learned from an experience dealing with black magic, and offers the reader an example of what precedes and then follows in this treatise.

Some years ago when working on a client's flat to resolve geopathic stress, he asked if I could help a friend of his who was experiencing an ongoing situation where no one, including a Buddhist monk expert in hauntings and similar, had managed to be of assistance.

It is rare to encounter such low energy in a person, the haggard look from constant lack of sleep, the haunted regard from very present fear, the shiftiness of rapidly moving eyes but short attention span. A walking wreck and not even 50 years old! He felt confident enough to tell me his tale which was startling, to say the least. A very successful business marketing FDA-approved homeopathics until four years ago when a series of events caused total collapse of his health, the business and basically everything he touched. On one of my visits, I actually witnessed pigeons walk into his flat through a mezzanine floor window and crap on his little altar, as well as elsewhere before he shooed them away and closed the window which he swore had been shut – he had done enough cleaning up to know their antics!

He believed the origin of all these misfortunes was a former employee, a white South African, who practised black magic and accomplished his misery with the help of a disembodied entity under his control. Peter was regrettably familiar with this entity as it had become an intimate member of his entourage, disrupting his sleep, provoking uncontrollable emotions and totally strange behavioural patterns. Suicidal tendencies, depression followed in quick succession with rare moments of respite.

Having heard him through on this first meeting, I asked if I might check his flat for "energy". The building was subject to geopathic stress, which is normal enough in Chiang Mai, but casting the net wider than normal, I checked where the pendulum indicated a source of low energy, his front door was off the charts. By this time I was using a chart of my own fabrication with all information useful to me incorporated. The reading was -55 compared with -15 or so inside the apartment itself.

Back again the following day to install the rods, thinking that the safest way of proceeding was to consolidate the environmental energy before trying any possible treatment I took a Polaroid photo of him so as to work on his case quietly at home in what I believed to be the safety of my office. Seriously and unwittingly out of my depth as I was soon to discover, but naively fearing nothing due to a sense of "wanting to help", we parted company with the plan to meet up again soon.

Little did I know! My wife and I spent a sleepless night, in absolute terror and disarray. The ghastly face of whatever it was moved constantly around the bedroom, one instant up so close it seemed to move through my own body, the next, hovering over a statue on the table near the window, making it move. I have no recollection of a body, just the head, consisting of colours, pastel and faded, features distorted in what one can only be termed hate, anger and pain, and the extraordinary ability to convey those feelings that left me in a complete and utter fear. Remembering what little I knew of sorcery and such, every effort went into visualizing an intense blue-white light, trying to spread it in a protective blanket around us both. In the moments of respite when the 'thing' temporarily gave up its frenzied action, I tried to calm the fear as well I could, reasoning that energetically it is no different from me, therefore, pure energy – love. I then attempted to communicate that message of being at one or unicity with the entity.

This seemed to keep it at a little distance but there was no question of letting up on the effort, for as soon as that mindset eased up, back surged the face in the most gruesome of rages immediately in front of me.

OTHER-DIMENSIONAL ENTITIES

Even the most terrifying of demonic deities depicted in the Tibetan Buddhist pantheon pale beside this excruciating horror which finally let up as the dawn appeared. Events had been so mesmerizing and attention so focussed on keeping it all together rather than giving in to the desire to run, but where? Perhaps it was also fear for the children in the room across the corridor that kept us both riveted, but that was just an impression, I was glued to the bed. One of those brief episodes that lasts for ever.

Severely shaken, exhausted and in considerable doubt as to what to do next, I asked a series of questions with the pendulum, and took the Polaroid photo of my new 'friend' to a nearby river and dropped it in with a prayer for it to flow to the ocean, and then on through the water cycle to the sky and the light. Back home, a lot more questioning followed oriented around possible protective measures, whether I should let things be and declare forfeit, or if there is anything to be done.

Whatever it was that happened, if it was to frighten me – it worked! Logically speaking if the intention was to hurt, it could have caused my heart to seize, so intense was the apprehension, so more likely a warning to back off and go play elsewhere. For I am quite convinced that whatever it was, it had that kind of power.

I related all this to Peter on the phone, he was not surprised by this performance and even made light of it saying "Now you know what I have been living with for four years!"

Feeling totally out of my depth I contacted a Jesuit priest I had met a few years previously and with whom I thought there might be a sympathetic ear at least, and at best, permission from the bishop to perform an exorcism. That was not to be. The dialogue basically never happened, the priest's initial suggestion was that I was psychologically overwrought and my imagination was running wild. That may well be I conceded, but it is not mine but someone else's life that is in danger, should the church not intervene if requested. Eventually on realising that I was sincere he said on his return from the Holy Land in three months he would contact the bishop if still necessary. I left on the parting shot that that would very probably be too late.

Feeling very isolated, unsure and apprehensive but with a little fight left, I worked the pendulum some more and Peter agreed to the course of action indicated. Using the "negative green" frequency, patented by de Bélizal and Chaumery, as generated with their Universal Pendulum in the electromagnetic phase, the idea was to cast out the entity attached to Peter into the river and away, like the photo.

So down to the Ping river, a quiet spot on the bank out of the public view, we prepared ourselves, each in his own manner, and the pendulum gyrated and swung for a few minutes. We parted company, he back to his flat a short distance away, and me back home to Huay Sai.

Two days later I phoned him as there had been no word from his end. He had been out for the count for two full days following the clearing, incapable of anything but the simplest of physical tasks, and was so angry at what I had done, he told me in no uncertain terms to leave him alone.

A short while later I received an unfriendly email from a "healer" friend of his in Canada. He had neglected to tell me that she was also working on protecting him, but she told me that I should have checked for her presence in the equation before proceeding, as I had knocked her out for several hours before she understood what was going on. Miffed at being treated in such a manner by two people I did not know from Adam, especially as I had paid quite heavily for something I did not ask for, it was easy to call it a day. It took a little time for me to understand that was perhaps a normal reaction in the circumstances and in any case, better to assume that viewpoint and not be judgemental.

Twenty months later he contacted me again, apologising and asking if there was anything I could do given the only relief he ever had was when I had worked on him. Hmmm! Do I want more of the same? Just how masochistic can one get? He was still possessed by this evil entity, business was even worse, his health wretched, pigeons just as brazen, now laying eggs galore on his balconies of the twenty-sixth floor!

In between times, my methods had evolved and learning expanded. By that time I had learned of the Atlantis symbol, and was using it as psychic protection. It came into immense use and I dare say, changed Peter's life. The immediate solution was to place one of the symbols at the foot and head of his bed, which allowed him to get some sleep. The entity was unable to penetrate the magnetic field created by the symbols and he could see her – for it was still the same female ghoul – trying to break through as she moved in every direction around the field. A visiting friend had found him sleep-walking dangerously close to the unprotected balcony at two in the morning and had, with difficulty, managed to get him back to bed, where at least he found some respite shielded by the symbols.

The Kahuna tradition of Hawaii has an interesting history of magic according to Max Freedom Long and this gave me the inspiration as to how to possibly deal with these entities who fulfil the commands of those desperate enough to stop at nothing to achieve their ends. The Kahuna magician apparently closes with the entity and convinces it that the target does not have what they are after, but the controller does and they send the entity back and, due to the controller's lack of protection perhaps caused by the arrogance of power, lose their lives at the hand of their minion. There were far too many questions in my mind as to how this might work out so that Peter would survive, let alone how to deal with the frustration of the magician and his recruit.

You know when you start down a certain path but can never be sure where it will lead. This radical Kahuna solution was not my cup of tea, reeking of unhappy karma.

But what if one contacted the spirit entity and worked a deal?

I took another photo of Peter and sure enough the entity came with it but did not bother Cat this time, just me. Not anyone's idea of fun but it allowed me to establish a form of communication and I suggested an exit from all this misery for the entity, whose name I learned, by offering a way to the light and release from what must be rather a miserable way of passing one's existence. The pendulum remained without a response, because that was how I chose to communicate – I did not have the courage to confront the entity one on one!

There was a belief in ancient Egypt whereby you can gain considerable power over someone if you know their name, much like having their image or photo, I believe. Every day I asked the entity, by name, and it was a female, if she was ready to leave this world of ours. No reply, and I was beginning to question this process but managed to overcome my natural impatience. A week later, sensing her presence in my office I asked the question once again, the answer was yes! She was ready to leave to the light, and the method I suggested with the special frequency pendulum was good. I took the opportunity to ask some questions about the world she had worked in for thousands of years to learn some tricks of the trade before she left, which she graciously answered.

Peter's relief was immense, but he was sceptical as past experience had been bitter, but he now had an Atlantis ring, which needed some improvement in the design but sufficient to afford protection from further psychic attack in case the South African gent still had control over other entities to throw at him. Apparently that was the case but not until some few years later, but that is another story. What is important was that Peter recovered his health, his will to live and to a certain extent his business.

It was a steep and cruel learning curve but one which has proved very useful in numerous similar instances, because as mentioned previously, black magic seems to be the flavour of the day.

What is more alarming in the statistics mentioned below is the increasing number of people involved in the black arts, and that seems to be throughout the world. If you become involved in this work of spirit release, it is inevitable that you will sooner or later be confronted with cases of possession/obsession due to this sordid practice.

Using the colour chart provided below, and I would strongly recommend you develop your own as a function of your knowledge base and methodology, one is able to discover very rapidly who you are dealing with, revealing the true nature of the person, and consequently, be forewarned and forearmed.

The manner in which magicians work seems to be as a function of their ability, whatever, that is not our problem. As far as the person trying to help is concerned, there is considerable advantage in knowing as precisely as possible who and what one is dealing with. There is a real danger, however, of escalation if you, as the release-worker, take things personally or assume a position of righteousness. You can only be of assistance if neutrality is maintained, compassion for all concerned is a given. The focus must be on the release of the entities, for there might be more than one involved. The entity is the energy form causing the harm – albeit on another person's instructions, the possessed is the direct medium for all action and the vector for the release process, but the other dimensional entity is the cornerstone. Release the entity, there is relief for the victim and one less tool for the magician.

Before moving on to the issue of curse, we might take a look at the most evil of the magical efforts going on in the world today – and perhaps for a great while longer, as it seems that sacrifice, especially child sacrifice has been around for a long time.

A child is worth a million US dollars according to a reliable source involved in the trafficking business. Depending on which end of the economic scale one is located, that could be a great deal, or a mere bagatelle. Given that the majority of humankind is at the lower end of the scale, it is tempting to become involved in this miserable game.

Establishments of education and religion are the two most easily accessible, and in the first instance, compulsory passageways for children in their very slow evolution into the adult world. I say slow because compared to the animal world, where one risks losing your life if you cannot run, and run fast, within a day or two of arriving in this world, the child is not independent for many years, requiring protection and care all the time. Yet one hears very little from the school or church about this very real danger for kids.

A commonly used method in the child-grooming domain is black magic. By targeting a fragile family, especially a single mother, the predator can soften up the intended victim(s) using an unsophisticated other dimensional entity to wreak havoc in the life, imagination and environment of the target. We can help by removing these entities, for while such cases may be a minority compared to the number of children who disappear every year throughout the world, generally never to be heard from again, we can contribute a little to removing this contamination.

There is no suggestion here that you try to infiltrate the local coven, but rather that you keep an eye open in your clearing work for any untoward signs of such dark activity.

Some years ago, I mentioned to a very talented frequency medicine therapist my family was consulting that the consulting rooms of the practice were over geopathic stress, and I would happily resolve that issue if so desired. On the elected day, another person joined me, having been requested to help with the many animals present, especially horses. The energy readings in the stables of the first property were dismal. The horses were nervous and jittery, apparently hesitant about crossing into the yard after being out in the pasture. Sure enough, there was quite some entity presence, and the atmosphere improved after clearing in a number of areas. The person told me of a burial ground a few hundred metres away, unused today but in past centuries used to bury unbaptised children, born out of wedlock and sometimes unwed mothers. Several hundred entities went off to the light in that one session, and I then returned to the main house.

There was an unusually high negative reading on the outside of the house immediately after installing the device to counter the geopathic stress, which in itself was very strange. While checking for a possible reason for that, I was called urgently from the stables across the muddy paddock. Running to discover what had caused the alarm, the two people were in a state of what I can only describe as shock. They had seen and felt a shadowy presence pass behind them as they stood outside the box of the horse they were discussing, the mare had shied away so violently she had broken the skin as she cowered against the wall, where she now stood and refused to budge. Once again the readings on my chart were extremely low, and even after another clearing with the Karnak pendulum, my tool of predilection for this type of work, they improved until reaching the box at the end of the stable, when the lowest possible reading was indicated. A large billy goat was housed in there. A fine specimen with eyes that gave me the distinct impression that I was not in the right place, and not at all welcome. Only on returning home and alone in the calm of my office when I checked the therapist's colour again with the pendulum whilst using a special mudra with the other hand, that the penny dropped. I was being played.

Discretion is an essential saving grace in this business, and probably what is even more important is the gift of perception that can guide you. One is not trying to develop power, merely to avoid suffering for others and oneself, and that requires a subtle mix of humility, determination and the recognition that others might be far more powerful than the force that you trust is there to protect you. A slow navigation in trial and error seems to be the only way to spare yourself a world of trouble. There is no point confronting that force of evil, it can extinguish you like a candle, but is unable to resist love, the sole remedy. If you cannot bring love to bear in such a situation, neutrality has to be maintained but is no guarantee of safety and sanity. It is not our job to put things to right, the whiff of ego in doing that can be your undoing. That is not the role of the white magician, our fragile light must never be tarnished by a <u>desire</u>, even if it is to help, however tempting.

For several years in Bangkok, a substantial number of Indian Sikh families called upon my services ranging from getting rid of demonic entities, rectifying geopathic stress, releasing the spirits of murdered relatives, working on other dimensional entities, and predicting fortune or otherwise (which I sometimes foolishly did!), to divining the decisions of the judges in their multi-million lawsuits, which seemed to occupy much of their energy and waking time. The black magicians of the Punjab are in a class apart is the conclusion that I came to, because of the almost constant referral made by these urbane, westernised, wealthy (for the most part) Indians to these compatriots of theirs to help them in their mundane needs. Apart from the sordid legal aspect where only the lawyers fattened themselves on the proceeds, there was a very dark side involving murder, suicide, possession, wretched physical suffering worked by the magicians paid substantial sums to work their misery. I was quite naïve in getting involved, and lucky to come out unscathed.

CHAPTER 9
CURSE

The extreme case of Peter recounted above, cursed by an employee who used a very malevolent other dimensional entity to plague his life and ruin his business, is not a rare event in human affairs. In a single period of three years for example, I encountered four similar instances, of varying degrees of intensity, all resulting from curse motivated by greed, but all using black magic in the attempt to achieve the objective.

One naturally acquires a reputation over time for being involved in this obscure universe, and it is only thanks to that exposure that one gains partial insight to some of the aspects that prevail. For the victims of a hex, spell or curse, it is well worth assessing the resilience and ability to resist of the individual, because one must have the person's confidence and trust if you are to be of any use.

On several occasions when living in the north of Thailand, I arrived too late, either at the hospital or in the hill-tribe village, to be of use clearing the patient. So firm is the belief that death or horrible outcome will follow, that the victim gives up instantly offering no resistance. There can be no doubt that we are subject to our own imaginations in this, and probably other, respects.

Of the four instances mentioned above, it was possible to connect with all save one of the entities involved. The 'miss' was a Japanese, so deeply immersed in the horror and total desperation, that it was nigh on impossible to connect with him, let alone the invading entity. The other three cases were European males, two of whom knew who had instigated the process against them, and were resisting.

In most cases, the victim is initially unaware of anything untoward, but the earlier one is able to detect interference from a third party the

OTHER-DIMENSIONAL ENTITIES

better, for obvious reasons. Depending on the means at the disposal of the magician, the victim's life can be made a little chaotic, or outright demonic. In the latter case, questioning with the pendulum can determine if relief is possible or if death is imminent. As in all walks of life, being street-wise is sensible, although there is no doubt that it is quite startling to learn that you are on someone's hit list.

The sequence of events, generally but not necessarily in order, seems to affect health, relationships, equipment, business, impressions/emotions. Life is inclined to deteriorate fast, with mystery diseases or health conditions where doctors are incapable of diagnosing let alone curing; severe upsets in business dealings and unexplainable mishaps of all sorts; out-of-the-blue breakdowns in close relationships, even of a mechanical nature; sentiments and emotions that overwhelm and override one's habitual values and standards… The list may be never ending, and of course, unique to every individual subject to this plague.

As already stated, it is best to keep that kind of contact as distant as possible, because the aggression and animosity are ferocious; impossible for a 'normal' individual to contemplate, let alone overcome alone. For the victim, however, there is nothing but uncertainty, so faith and conviction are as important as being obstinate and bloody-minded! It is generally easier said than done, but to keep the agent at arm's length is a very good idea.

If one is called in to help in these situations, which I would add are common but of so many different forms, there can be no relevant advice which I would be able to offer beyond the obvious. Listen carefully, question everything (only if you have the means to obtain reliable answers), especially whether you should get involved. I would add here that there are problem people who thrive on the mystery and drama; their problems are real but diplomacy is necessary as it is easy to push certain people too far, and you can be caught in the aftermath. An amazing learning is guaranteed, but remember that survival is a razor's edge!

The obvious for me is compassion, love – as in another's experience becomes your own if shared, and if it is the way and design of the Superior Intelligence, then graceful acceptance smooths the way, and an exit can be found.

Practically speaking, your effort can be best oriented to convincing the invading other dimensional entity that one is concerned for their well-being, and that you are there to help them as well. Having

Chapter 9

established that the other dimensional entity is indeed present, the connection is made. Depending on your approach but especially on what you find you are dealing with – in much the same way as one conducts negotiations – a position of firmness and equanimity allows you to affirm your presence in no other role than that of providing relief. The entity is most probably very aware of their considerable responsibility in causing the problem(s) by working for someone who wants to cause mischief, but that is not the objective. The greatest appeal for the mischief-making other dimensional entity would appear to be its salvation. One can only presume the psychological impact at play, but it has apparently worked in every instance I have encountered once that connection is made.

The great advantage of this is to remove the magician's cat's paw, without any confrontation, and with no appeal possible, because the other dimensional entity has opted of its own free will for the light and an exit from the sordid side. That is probably part of what one might entitle the free will process, whereby we are able to refuse evil as being detrimental to our own well-being.

The frustration of the magician is the risk one must run, but I would venture the guess that their energy is better employed in finding a new recruit and training them up, rather than hunting the culprit down. I sincerely hope so!

Consideration could well be given to the power of thought, it would appear to be severely underestimated, mainly because we are not taught really how to think effectively and even less about the possibility of directing that electromagnetic frequency, which we are told thought is made up of, in a constructive way. But when you appreciate that every action one undertakes in life is the sequence of an impulse originating in the heart, which then leads to achieving the object of one's desire, the process can be appreciated as not only conclusive but most effective.

There are degrees of curse, and once again careful questioning with the pendulum will help you find out how hot the water actually is. There will always be someone stronger than the next person (you), so conflict is out of the question to my mind, not from any moral basis, but purely as an expedient. Better to find another way out, and there always is, however obscure.

In Thailand, where life is not held in high regard, and can be dispensed with remarkably cheaply, it is common to find the local black magician, the *po mut* – father of the ants, ready to do the bidding of whoever is prepared to pay two thousand baht (52 euros at current rates). That could include a number of "services", elimination being one of them. Neither timing nor death is guaranteed, whereas suffering is, with death a distinct possibility, as I often saw with hill-tribe folk. I have no idea what the cost is in the western world, most likely far more, but that is of little consequence. What is important is the very fact that people are prepared to do this kind of work for money, and will stop short of nothing. Can you imagine explaining that to your local police officer, let alone bringing an end to such pure evil?

CHAPTER 10
METHOD OF ANALYSIS

I developed this unique method of diagnosis using colours on the basis of the work made in the 1930s by André de Bélizal and Leon Chaumery when they first found that frequencies – to which they attributed colours – emanate from a scale model of the Cheops pyramid. They decided that referring to colours rather than frequencies was a more eloquent manner of sharing their findings. I experimented on the basis of further research by other radiesthesists, Enel (Michel Skariatine), Turenne, Luzy, de la Foye, my Polish monk acquaintance, and gradually refined this system. But first, a little background might help to consolidate the logic.

Although photons apparently originate in and reach us from the sun, it is only when they reach the earth's atmosphere that they become what we know as light because the vibrational frequencies are transformed to that end by the unique combination of qualities present in the atmosphere, such as pressure, temperature and motion. This is but a small part of the story of the many invisible frequencies that impact the earth from the universe; however, the colours are what we are most aware of because they play such an important role in our lives. We are perhaps not so aware that the reason for the specific colours we see are due to the wavelengths of those frequencies, with the colour green, the "colour" of the energy form originating from the sun, having a peak wavelength of 0.45 micrometers. So what we in fact see is a function of the energy form, not the colour *per se*.

A possible parallel could be drawn with astrology, in which the influence of the planets and their energetic frequencies have a certain bearing on human life and behaviour, thanks to the combined terrestrial and cosmic energies at play during the life of the individual. Given that every person has his or her own specific frequential pattern, which can reasonably be assumed to be an aggregate frequency of their cellular vibration, it is but a step to categorize those vibrations into colour so as to form a practical method that can be readily applied.

The origins of these frequencies are multiple, cosmic and telluric, ancestral perhaps, even immediate in that they come from the intake of food and drink of the mother, and so on, but they could be regarded as frequencies in seed form of the individual's life purpose, much like an acorn or plant seed.

This broad spectrum was what de Bélizal, Chaumery, and Paul-André Morel were working on, and they found that a number of objects, both natural and manufactured — trees, certain buildings of special geometric architecture, spherical objects — contain a spectrum of colours. Having found that a half-sphere, as indeed the pyramid, generates a spectrum of 48 frequency colours, they experimented and soon found that a collection of identical half-spheres set up in series and arranged in a sphere can both project and detect the frequency of the "colour" in question when positioned on a specific axis and equator, but that is not the point here.

The reason for considering this phenomenon is purely practical. This aggregate energetic colour in an individual is a simplification of the notion whereby one assumes that the multiple components found in a being can be categorized into a readily understandable scale. It is a matter of fitting people into a box, in much the same way biologists, geneticists and anthropologists do. Nothing strange or esoteric should be read into this fact, a person simply has a colour attributed as a function as to how they fulfil their life. This is the colour referred to in the character analysis that I practice. It is an extremely practical and simple way of determining an individual's state of health or otherwise, because, ideally, this colour should be identical to the individual's internal colour (the sum of all psychosomatic components) for the person to be in balance. The external physical colour is indicative of much more, however, as we shall see later.

The hypothesis here is that an individual's "external physical colour" is a frequential manifestation. I would hasten to add that this has no relation to the "aura" as revealed by Dr. Walter Kilner, which, when applied by him, is an indication of the individual's organic condition along the lines of thermography.

All external colours referred to here are in the electric phase, probably because it originates from the heart's electrical impulse, and what I refer to as the "internal" colour, is of a magnetic nature.

The colour generally does not change during the life of an individual but can still be detected from a photograph of a person or from his or her name and date of birth, an item of clothing, or some other item even after physical death. Under some circumstances, the colour can change during a person's lifetime, but that will be discussed at a later stage.

Obviously, humans are not the only beings that share this colour-frequency manifestation. Everything does, which is what the physicist school of dowsing picks up on. Water also contains this frequency, in the electric phase too, but it is more an indication of the water's maturity, therefore quality. All animals, from the ant to the elephant are found to be of the colour green. The subject of another hypothesis no doubt, but not for now.

These colours are in close relation to the human makeup, an impression of their aggregate quality, but not to be confused with the emotional, spiritual, mental, and physical states, which can be determined with reference to the internal colour, as such components are subject to constant change as experienced in the ups and downs of daily life.

In the same way that what we see with our eyes is a very limited portion of what is actually there because our eyes only pick up the narrow frequency waveband, and maybe even act as a filter for the brain, providing sufficient information for the immediate need only, likewise perhaps everything we gather through our many antenna senses has this same capacity to conceal an immensity of potentiality that is unknowingly tapped into, but ignored except for the immediate necessity. It would make sense that this "mechanism" is one of survival, and what a masterpiece. But what does it imply for the larger picture of existence and its way of operation—the domain of knowledge?

External colours

Individual people are associated with one of six colours, which, as mentioned earlier, generally stays with the person his or her entire life. A number of immensely useful indications can, however, be gleaned

OTHER-DIMENSIONAL ENTITIES

from these colours, which are:

- White,
- Violet,
- Indigo,
- Blue,
- Green,
- Black.

It is now time to tread warily, for we are on thin ice, being in the domain where nothing can be categorically posited, but everyday experience confirms a consensus sentiment.

The main characteristics of these colours are as follows:

- White is a manifestation of harmony; "white" people are few and far between. The individual becomes white as a result of effort; I believe that people are not born with this colour. It is useful to categorize this further on a scale of 1-10.

- Violet people are not alone in their vital space; these are the 'possessed' individuals who concern us the most. What is intriguing is that they often have a mission in their life, generally not their own, but of the invading entity, nothing will get in their way in their determination to accomplish that objective, which is what makes the urgency in dealing with them, if possible. Some famous examples include Mahatma Gandhi, Mother Teresa, Joseph Stalin, Adolf Hitler, Pol Pot, Cecil Rhother dimensional entities, and Mao Zedong. This violet colour changes once the "personality" is cleared.

- Indigo indicates people who are more spiritually rather than materialistically oriented. It is one of the two colours found most commonly among "normal" people, those who labour as best they can, doing what they believe is in the best interests of one and all. The *shen* are in predominance in indigo people's behaviour, and although the *hun* and *po* are active, they do not generally get out of hand resulting in excess.

Chapter 10

- Blue is a commonly found colour. Blue people are much in keeping with indigo but with the difference that the *po* are inclined to gain the upper hand, and behaviour is more material-oriented. These people are more readily subject to excess than indigo persons, but with their heart in the right place with regard to others nevertheless.

- Green is very rare in humans; I have only ever found it in one individual, whose brain was severely impaired as the result of a motorbike accident.

- Black is the colour of persons dominated by material desire and the urge to achieve their aim at any cost. This is not a good condition to be in; it is very unhealthy for persons hosting the colour as well as for those in their presence, although the former are unlikely to notice, let alone be bothered. People imposing their will on others due to overwhelming egoism are of this colour. To avoid being sued for defamation, I will name no examples, but they are numerous and found in all walks of life; black people are increasingly common, especially in the political class. This is an acquired colour; people are not born in this condition but deliberately opt for it. The predominant emotions manifested by such people are hate and anger in one form or another. Using a scale of 1-10 one can discover the true nature of the person and the degree of evil practised.

Animals and plants, without exception, do not share this colour scheme in its diversity; they are all green, systematically.

The purpose of this colour scheme is primarily for analysis; it is not a score sheet intended to judge people, so be careful of reading too much into its interpretation, although it is very useful to know what kind of person one is dealing with. The analysis is based on the balance (or imbalance) of external and internal colours; if both external and internal colour are the same, all well and good, but if not, there is imbalance, and further investigation is necessary to find where the problem lies. It is a remarkable way to help establish harmony in individual existence.

Internal Colours

These colours are: red, orange, yellow, blue, indigo, plus white, black, and negative green.

OTHER-DIMENSIONAL ENTITIES

Having determined the person's external colour, one then asks what the internal colour is. If identical to the external, all well and good, but if not, there is imbalance. As mentioned above, if the individual is externally violet, the first thing to do is to release the other dimensional entity(ies). The colour will then change to their own intrinsic colour.

The yellow colour is generally due to an organic issue affecting the liver, the seat of the *hun*, or the lung. Orange indicates poison, possibly the mother-in-law, alimentary intoxication, or some other externally caused problem such as from an insect bite or sting. Red indicates emotion or extreme fatigue. Black is a danger sign indicating a critical situation on the cusp, which can either revert back to harmony or flip to negative green, which is very critical.

Chinese *feng shui* practitioners use a tool called a *bagua* (*pakua*), a circular device with a basis of eight trigrams, to analyze energy and its manifestation; it also has a colour scheme corresponding to the trigrams, but that is another kettle of fish.

This brings us to a question which risks never being unanimously resolved.

Is there not something immaterial that remains after the physical death of the body?

The answer is very much dependent on one's understanding of material. If the material has no other origin than the spirit, the answer is easy. If the material has intrinsic reality, it will evolve and the answer changes. The propositions in answer to this question are no doubt of interest and although probably not to be contained in a single volume, I address the magnetic aspect in the final appendix to this book.

What if this is a fundamental biomagnetic expression, a function of the life energy, the Chinese *qi* or the Vedic *prana*? We know that the strength of such an element in a living human varies according to different factors — exposure to electromagnetic radiation, the strength or otherwise of the immune system, the wearing of shoes, environmental influences, physical sickness, emotional well-being, and so on.

If, in the final analysis, a human entity is a vast batch of frequencies, it seems quite natural that the biomagnetic component persists after the death of the physical envelope, and it could well be the basis for the belief that "something" of the person-specific frequencies survives.

Time perhaps to look at what other traditions and cultures have to say on the subject.

CHAPTER 11
TEXTUAL AUTHORITY

To my knowledge, there is no written text in our modern tradition that explains the passage from life to death, nor the inverse, should there be a continuity to existence here on the plane of earth as experienced by mankind and whatever it is we are made of. Modern science cannot help us because totally persuaded of the reality of the material alone.

Even in the texts from ancient traditions, most of the time we have to deal with allusions; the *bhur*, *bhuvar* and *svar* in India (in Sanskrit these are three of the seven worlds or aspects of creation, the three regions of mortals, intermediate space and heaven, especially pronounced in rituals); the *hun* and *po* in China; the *ka*, *ba*, etc. in Egypt; soul and spirit in Christian texts, and so on. There is no apparent clearcut description or explanation of what and how it is all about. Reputedly, the Druids did not commit to paper, nor did the American Indians, neither did the Australian Aborigines, albeit for historically different reasons, yet those groups appear to have strong spiritual backgrounds to their ways of being.

India

A unique insight from the Hindu tradition to normally invisible dimensions is to be found in Chapter XI of the Bhagavad Gītā, as translated by Swami Pranav Tirtha's *Living the Gita*, from the Introduction:

"This fascinating story of the mighty Me's pervasiveness inside and outside everything, and the picture of all and everything being

OTHER-DIMENSIONAL ENTITIES

Me, aroused in Arjuna [the protagonist in this story], as it would in all Arjunas even today, a strong desire for visual demonstration. God is not and cannot be an object of the senses, or even the mind. The Upanishads as well as common-sense say as much; if he were, he would be anything but God. But if Krshna could conjure up in Arjuna's mind such an impressive picture, why not ask him? People ask more only of those who can and do give; not the have not or the niggardly. Where then was the harm in asking Krshna [avatar of Vishnu, playing the role of Arjuna's chariot-driver], who was neither? Arjuna knew what Krshna indeed was. He had no doubt this miracle of a man could manage miracles. Past master in psychic lore and its practice, naturally clairvoyant, ESP was child's play to him; and what we call hypnotism, being only a part of the yogic art of exploring other people's minds came to him easily. If the power of suggestion and the subject's willingness were to be helpful factors, well, the latter was there in abundance, and the former had already been accomplished in Chapter X.

This all goes to indicate that the innumerable and diverse energy forms experienced by man are the adjuncts of Maya (the cosmic play of illusion) in its temporo-spatial facet – but VERY REAL.

And that is the problem here, these forms are real yet defy our understanding of reality.

Especially as we tend to anthropomorphise things, i.e. give events, beings, thoughts and whatever else the human mind can conjure up, a form, very often closely followed by a name, so that we can relate.

As demonstrated above, there is no particular form to energy, but it assumes what the individual is capable of conceptualising. This is very much the case of what we find in the domain of what are colloquially referred to as 'entities'.

There is a topic that I think is worth taking a closer look at before we tackle that subject; incarnation.

Rebirth is a purely human construct that has nothing whatsoever to do with the reality of Oneness. We would do well to recall that fact.

Evolution is surely the principal inspiration and necessary motivation for humanity, at the origin of so much that humankind has achieved. Humans, whether primitive or sophisticated, are apparently the only creatures who manifest a belief in this compelling idea, to surpass the human condition of physicality based on the conviction that there is something more than what we actually see. That belief then finds numerous forms of expression in human activity, generally supported by a philosophical or religious doctrine.

Among these systems, the Hindu doctrine of karma is unique in that it includes an inbuilt morality and sense of responsibility, devoid of any guilt complex or subservience. Volumes have been written to explain the workings of karma and, by extension, the theory of Nature's functioning, but little concerning the story of 'reincarnation'.

It would be foolish to discount this concept of 'reincarnation' out of hand, there are far too many accounts of memories of past lives from living people around the world, in diverse traditions and over lengthy periods of time. I think there is room for deeper insight. We need to consider that this frequently encountered and appealing idea <u>cannot</u> subsequently infer that reincarnation is systematic for all humans, in all places, and at all times. As a result this extraordinary evidence needs to be examined closely before assuming a potentially categoric stance.

There can presumably be no argument that in the course of a human lifetime a vast bank of impressions is accumulated, some of which might well leave an indelible trace, or such a forceful emotion, that then requires a reaction. That is what happens whilst living, in the awake state, but that surely does not mean that death of the physical brings a conclusion to those powerful impressions. Here is what the Hindus have to say in this respect:

It is said in the Mundaka Upanishad (3.2.2) – a section of the Atharva Veda, "Whoever hankers after desirable things while brooding on their qualities, is born in an environment conducive to and with those desires. But for the person whose desires are fully satisfied, freed of ignorance and established in true knowledge, all cravings vanish even here."

This would imply that a strongly held desire, irrespective of its inherent vice or quality, as of the time that it absorbs much of one's attention is sufficient to become a major factor in the continuation of one's evolutionary existence. So, if one associates with such desires, probably without any limitation of number, let alone possible cutoff in the degree of intensity, one might well – somehow or other – carry them through into a subsequent existence, in order to work them out – or not. What an incredibly fair deal!

Is this not what might well constitute the soul? A bundle of impressions with unresolved issues to deal with. One could well say that it is a return to square 1. The hard school of life which teaches us that the riddle can only be resolved by identification with the physical or the spiritual. Our free will is limited to that stark choice. Do you want to persist with the potentially endless circus of phenomenal experience – the whirligig of sensational stimulation?

Or, would you care for the peace and calm that underlies it all?

Your call.

If the Self is identified with desires, they can be achieved without much ado, even if additional physical existences are necessary to accomplish them. This is further confirmed in the Brhadaranyaka Upanishad (4.4.6): "In this respect, there is this verse: 'Being attached, the person, together with the karma, achieves that which the mind is attached to. Having exhausted the results of the work accomplished in this life, he returns from that world to this for further karma.' So it is for the person who desires, but the person free of desire, who has recognized that objects of desire are no different from your Self, is released from this attachment and remains merged in Brahman."

There does seem to be a considerable lack of understanding concerning the various theories of rebirth because we are inclined to express our rather vague beliefs in terms that approximate our comprehension. This may appear to be splitting hairs, but in fact it is of special relevance regarding the subject in hand, and to acquire a firmer understanding of these various concepts of rebirth, it is worth reading:

René Guénon (1886-1951), a French polymath and self-styled traditionalist, who clearly explains in *Theosophy: History of a Pseudo-Religion*, reincarnation, or the assuming of a physical form animated by a set of ideas preformed by past experience, is a relatively recent idea invented in Europe. In all likelihood, it was not originally proposed as "rebirth" as such but more as an apology, explanation, and potential means to achieve social justice, initiated by Gotthold Lessing in the second half of the eighteenth century and then developed further by the French socialists in the 1830–1840s (Charles Fourier, Pierre Leroux, and Henri de Saint-Simon), and subsequently fueled by Darwin's theory of evolution. Thus the ground was laid for a muddled theory combining the commonly held hope for man's betterment at some stage in the future, divine concern for justice, echoes of Judeo-Christianity, and finally, the recent arrival from the East, the doctrine of karma, which was rapidly interpreted as implying reincarnation due to a fuzzy

Chapter 11

notion of scientific cause-effect logic and an incomplete understanding of Eastern ideas further muddled by our Western strains of mysticism.

It seems appropriate here to mention that for Buddhism, there can be no question of reincarnation, for the simple reason that to incarnate there must be a connectivity provided by some kind of continuum entity, and Buddhists have none; there is no soul in Buddhism, the *anatta* doctrine is quite clear in that respect.

In Hinduism, the soul entity is provided for by the *jiva-atman* (aptly translated as "soul-spirit" by Dr. Sarvepalli Radhakrishnan), a notion totally lacking and denied in all schools of Buddhism.

In order to posit the idea of there being nothing permanent in the world, the Buddha developed a doctrine of relativity whereby everything is conditioned, relative, and interdependent. It goes by the name of Conditioned Genesis (*paticca-samuppada* in Pali) and consists of:

Avijjapaccaya samkhara: The cause of ignorance is the impressions.

Samkharapaccaya vinnanam: The cause of impressions is awareness (partially structured consciousness).

Vinnapaccaya namarupam: The cause of awareness is name and form.

Namarupapaccaya salayatanam: The cause of name and form is having intentions.

Salayatanapaccaya phasso: The cause of having intentions is sensual impression.

Phassapaccaya vedana: The cause of sensual impression is feeling.

Vedanapaccaya tanha: The cause of feeling is craving.

Tanhapaccaya upadanam: The cause of craving is grasping.

Upadanapaccaya bhavo: The cause of grasping is existence.

Bhavapaccaya jati: The cause of existence is birth.

Jatipaccaya jaramaranam: The cause of birth is death and decay.

While Buddhists consider this process as a cycle with twelve stages, number eleven breaking down into two, with birth resulting finally in death and decay, there is no mention of rebirth, merely a repetition of causes in the cycle of birth and death. The thread of continuity is enabled and created by the word *paccaya*, which means "having as a foundation," so insinuating an effect, but there is nothing to be read into this text that would suggest the potential development of another physical existence.

There is no such text in Hindu writings explaining so succinctly the cause of material existence and its continuity, but the Buddha (or his immediate followers) felt somewhat obliged to put things in order so as to propagate his teachings among students, thereby differentiating Buddhist beliefs from the Hindu paradigm of relative existence.

We, and I would include most people on the earth in that number, suffer from a serious illusion in believing reincarnation to be a Hindu doctrine. It is not, although it remains a possibility, inasmuch as there are not many metaphysical concepts that have not been considered in that vast sphere that we know as Hinduism. What is more, one could say that nothing is impossible and there is a strong chance of something happening if you invest sufficient energy into the belief that enables it. It is simply a matter of muddled conviction to assume that somehow the physical individual is alone at the origin of desire, without the means at the disposal of the all-one spirit. This does not imply that a human cannot form and achieve a desire, simply that it is not due to that combination, but rather thanks to the sublime system we experience.

Finally, a word about the frequently mistaken technical concepts of reincarnation, metempsychosis, and transmigration might be useful.

Reincarnation is the resuming of a new body by a being that has already assumed bodily form; unfortunately, there are no reliable texts explaining how this comes about, but it does require two conditions: a real and entire physical entity and a prior physical existence. Both are debatable metaphysically and scientifically, making reincarnation a tenuous issue, for who is to decide which of the mortal or imperishable elements go to make up the new body? The line between the psychic and corporeal elements is easily blurred, and it is this lack of clarity that causes the misconception among these terms. In reincarnation, both the conscious and the all-conscious images derived from sensory experience resulting in the imagination and memory can disappear with the fall of the first body, although not necessarily. The fact still remains that they are dependent on bodily existence in order to be manifested, and consequently are perishable because they can only arise in the conscious mind of an existing body.

Metempsychosis is an ancient belief expressed in the writings of Pythagoras and Plato (remember him, Aristotle's teacher, who also reputedly spent 13 years at school in Egypt), whereby it is believed that there are psychic elements in people that can be dispersed and are free to enter into other living forms, but not necessarily on the death of the body; they can migrate even while the "host" is alive. This is reminiscent of the behavior of the *po*. The difference lies in what are considered to be the mortal elements of the human, rather than the imperishable part—which is the real being or what I refer to as Consciousness, which is, in no way, impacted by any change. This condition also holds true for transmigration.

Transmigration is a change of state or passage of the real being to other states of existence. So, depending on your notion of real being, existence, and purpose, the answer lies in what it is that changes.

It seems opportune to leave this hotly debated subject there, for the individual to decide how they personally perceive change, but you can better understand why I say free will is limited to the choice of association – spirit or the physical.

The Christian dichotomy between man's free will and God's predisposition melts away when you realize that all is spirit!

OTHER-DIMENSIONAL ENTITIES

CHAPTER 12
DEALING WITH THE OTHER DIMENSIONAL ENTITY PHENOMENON

Does anyone tell us what to expect on the fall of the physical body? If we are lucky enough to have someone familiar with the various "Book of the dead" traditions, we can hope for some thanatological guidance as we pass over to the world of pure spirit. If not, we are very much left up to the vagaries of our education and immediate hazard.

The spectrum of reaction to physical death is probably limited, ranging from outright disbelief and refusal to accept the abrupt change, to shock and panic on finding the physical sheath is no longer, or quiet acceptance and reaching out to those hands proffered from the other side to guide the soul through the alarming experience – alarming for those convinced of the material reality of the "world".

That reaction in all likelihood determines the sequence of events, which is why it is not a bad idea to prepare for as smooth a transition as possible. If you are convinced of the reality of Consciousness (lucky

OTHER-DIMENSIONAL ENTITIES

you!), there is more of the same in store. If, on the other hand, the material body is the only "thing" you believe in, interesting times are around the corner and seemingly have to be gone through in order to learn and move on to a clearer understanding. The operative word is "clear", light or illumination being a characteristic of Consciousness, as anyone practising meditation will tell you.

Light, we are taught, in our physical world is an electromagnetic phenomenon and might be a key to the explanation of this luminous aspect of our intimate reality.

Our thanatological education is basically non-existent. No one, or remarkably few, in the modern western world is instructed as to how to deal with death, let alone guide those dying.

The key to whether the dying person takes the normal route – the tunnel to the light, accepting the extended hands and the calls, is, in all probability, a function of their mindset. If obsessed by concern for the welfare of the child, the house, the cat, and so on, there is a strong chance they will stay in the dimension where they no longer have their complete place, but they only discover that fact as a result of their refusal.

It then would appear to be too late, there is apparently no second chance. I say that because there seems little other explanation as to why this phenomenon of the other dimensional entity can persist. The sequel to that is anybody's guess, but among the anthropocentric hypotheses imaginable, one can well fancy that the errant spirit will probably find others in the same situation, and start a form of existence that can apparently only be terminated by encountering someone who can bring about their release. This last statement is obviously an interpretation, and merits being asked of an other dimensional entity when one has the opportunity.

This brings us to the crux of the subject. Is one human able to aid another in this very nebulous stage of an existence? Would it not be highly pretentious to make as if we can play at god when we don't even know what we are doing?

The answer of course is a resounding yes to both, even though that appears to be in absolute contradiction.

A human can help as of the time that the person is acting from the position of spirit. In exactly the same way that a Traditional Chinese

Chapter 12

Medicine practitioner operates. I'm not influenced by my patient's explanations, perhaps not even by their symptoms. Similarly, what I know is of no importance, the years of experience and books under the belt, the ego, all must be firmly placed to one side, and space cleared to allow communication of the protagonists – at the spiritual level.

This all sounds extremely vague, but if the intuition from your heart, in harmony with the *shen* (the 'cosmic' spirits), is in total accord with the All-conscious spirit, then you will be guided correctly.

The circumstances leading up to the moment of release are often full of synchronicity, as if we – the humans – are being manipulated to be in the right place, at just the right time to help them on their way. Why not?

The entities are the ones in need, and if it is your calling, and you have the mettle for the task, there is no option.

There are most probably a number of ways to help a discarnate entity move away from our earth dimension to the place where they should be in order to continue their journey. As we saw above, exorcism and hypno-therapy are seemingly the most common, but I question the efficiency especially of the former, as practitioners speak of attempting to remove the same entity from the same person repeatedly – it doesn't always work. If it is a battle of wills, then it is the practitioner versus the invading entity. If that other dimensional entity developed a strong will in their physical existence, it might well still be with them and a tussle is certain.

My desire, my intention is not what matters here, perhaps not even what the person with the entity wants either – as in cases of voluntary possession. The emphasis must be on the other dimensional entity, they are in the 'wrong' place, they need a solution to their predicament, and if we can provide it, we must do so using the most efficient and expedient method.

I use one only, a method confirmed as being the right one for me by the lady with whom I finally made friends mentioned above, and to whom this volume is dedicated. A carefully designed pendulum which generates a frequency that is used by the other dimensional entity to "travel" to the light.

The method I use is with a pendulum generating the negative green frequency in the electric phase, as defined and patented by de Bélizal and Chaumery. Boa Diya explained and confirmed to me that such a frequency can be used by an entity as a means of transport to the light. It strikes me as being not only suitable and adequate for an entity, in its disembodied, magnetic (?) state, to use a frequential path to exit this phenomenal dimension, rather than a wordy argument with good intentions thrown in. It is a subtle line that is drawn invisibly in our sands of understanding.

The distinct advantage of using a pendulum is that one is alone, there is no need to call upon the aid of others. Especially as a pendulum can also be used to clear remotely, when the situation allows.

A brief word on the procedure followed – as already said, it is generally the positive magnetic polarity hand over which the pendulum is placed, at a few centimetres above it. The pendulum starts gyrating, mostly clockwise for the benign entities, and frequently anti-clockwise for the malignant ones. The movement can be very strong, so one just has to hold on tight to the pendulum string, focussing mentally on the extraction to the light, wishing the entity peace and relief. In every case encountered, the pendulum completes it movement with a clockwise gyration.

It's as simple as that, but the ability to hold one's focus on the light of Consciousness while the pendulum is working away is very welcome.

One gets a very clear impression that the other dimensional entity knowing they are not in the right place, is now more than happy to move on. A neutral frame of mind, resting in a state of calm is the only recommendation I would offer.

Another reassuring item of information learned from my other dimensional entity informant was that an entity cannot return from the light to the physical dimension we currently experience. That was sufficient knowledge for me, and I did not pursue the matter further to ask further questions.

What happens next is an open book full of blank pages. There are no rules, no guidelines. Some people find instant relief and actually experience a sensation of being lighter, less oppressed; some turn on the waterworks; some feel nothing at all; some are suspicious and sceptical, and hold off before expressing any feeling. However, no one has ever asked for their money back!

Talking of which, it is not a bad idea to have a policy as regards clearing and possible payment. As a rule of thumb, I ask for nothing, but am more than happy to receive a contribution in some form or another, especially given that a clearing lasts about 45 seconds, so there is no correlation between the time of the task itself and monetary rate. Although, having said that, I sometimes experience a sensation of exhaustion that accompanies the work, which can be resolved in a variety of ways, especially 20 minutes in the orgone accumulator, but it does go, albeit slowly.

As stated elsewhere I am more concerned for the other dimensional entity. When time is spent on listening, counselling and clearing, then it is only fair to ask for a fee for your time, but such affairs can be addressed on an individual basis. How often has a client been incapable of paying? A little cup of kindness has a tendency to do the rounds.

The patient, in case of 'possession', can express their case, and one might be able to find solace through compassionate understanding, even resolution.

It is possible to converse with a patient, find alternatives and even laugh about it. Communication with an other dimensional entity is different, happening on a plane with which the physical human is on unfamiliar ground, in an unknown language, or rather no language, with beings who are sometimes in the most deplorable state, and I can only thank the superior intelligence that cares for me that I rarely see them. Simply being aware of their presence and offering to help them access the light of consciousness is generally sufficient to gain their confidence and acquiescence. Rare are the obstinate entities who do not want to leave their host when offered the opportunity, and fortunately, in my experience even that does not last for long.

The entities reluctant to leave are the ideal target for the black magician, as they share a dogged determination and are often very domineering. At an educated guess I would also venture those are the ones frequently inhabiting schizophrenics. One cannot help but wonder what happened to all the patients of 'mental' homes and clinics who were evicted as a result of Margaret Thatcher's healthcare act of the early 1980s when they were released into the community. As you can deduce from the above, I would be a strong advocate for the probable relationship between mental issues and other dimensional entity presence. Even if there was more research done, it would require a major sea change for the medical profession to acknowledge any kind of spiritual possibility, a complete removal of pharmaceutical control,

OTHER-DIMENSIONAL ENTITIES

and eradication of the profit-motive in exchange for good health.

CHAPTER 13
EASY RECOGNITION

Is it not irrational to expect to find answers to spiritual or metaphysical issues using physical logic? However, that is precisely what we do. And therefore it is scarcely surprising that we fall short of the truth, and the field is left wide open to the wildest of speculation, and inevitable manipulation by the unseemly mischief-makers of this world.

When using the method of analysis explained below, the first indication of an individual not being alone in their vital space is the violet external colour. With the person sitting in front of you, or remotely, with their photo, or name and date of birth on a piece of paper placed in the centre of the chart, one asks "What is the external colour of this person?"

In the same way as one discovers other dimensional entity presence due to the purple colour of the physical external colour in a person, clearance is confirmed when asking for the external colour once more, and it will be found to be any other colour than violet.

There does seem to be a common denominator with all people suffering from 'possession', and regrettably this is an increasingly prevalent condition, namely a weak magnetic field, but more on that later.

If the colour is found to be violet, the next question is "How many entities are there?", the pendulum will indicate on the scale of 0-10 the response. If there are more than ten, the pendulum will indicate the

OTHER-DIMENSIONAL ENTITIES

number in sequence.

Having found the person to be not alone, ask "Is this voluntary?" In other words, has the person in question deliberately allowed the situation to develop.

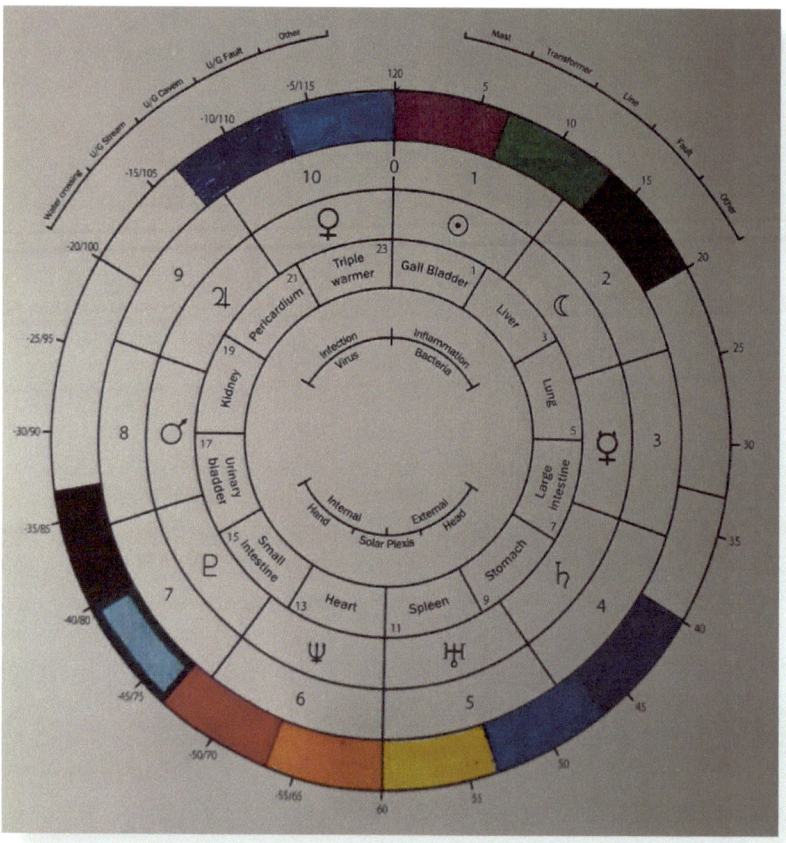

As a function of the answer to the question, "Is this voluntary?", one needs to ask if the person has been cursed, as the answer will determine whether you seek help, or if you are equipped to deal with the situation, are you doing so in as full awareness as possible.

The following series of questions would then be advisable:

- Is the entity happy to go to the light?
- Can I do the necessary?
- Can I do it now?
- Is this the right device to use? (holding the specific pendulum in hand).

If the answer is yes to all of the above, one proceeds with the protocol.

A word of caution

Here is a memorable quote from Malcolm Rae, one of the leading British figures in radionics: 'One of the most alarming features of Radiesthesia is the number of people who, finding some sort of response from a pendulum, believe themselves competent to use one, completely and accurately, whilst possessing nothing approaching the skill and reliability required for responsible use. There is something in common between learning to use the pendulum and learning to play the piano, in that skill comes only from an adequate amount of practise in doing each well.'

The message is especially true in the business of spirit release.

More so than in any other field, it is vital to maintain one's integrity based on values that are not for sale. The dangers are hard to imagine and are not just physical.

OTHER-DIMENSIONAL ENTITIES

CHAPTER 14
PERMISSION & ATTITUDE

There appear to be no rules as regards permission for release, but that is always something to be taken into account, otherwise one can end up assuming the rather dictatorial position of the exorcist, demanding banishment. As in life, courtesy is always appreciated, so I would extend the same civility to those involved, for it is a good idea to have the client and other dimensional entity onboard with the process. There are no doubt instances where one does have to be firm and insistent, but your own intuition and experience will surely show you the way.

Very often we believe that our conviction is sufficient, we then apply our intention to accomplish what we think is right, but would it not be fair and more just to ask if such is the right course of action?

For example, it is not generally a problem to convince someone that holding on to their mother is not a good idea, maybe even selfish, especially when the pendulum – or your method of accessing information – tells you the mother is fed up and wants out!

Once again, using the pendulum is a remarkably simple way of finding answers to questions of this nature. One asks if the other dimensional entity wishes to move on to the light; I would always suggest they invite any other entities in the vicinity if they would care to take the opportunity of tagging along. The state of mind of the practitioner at this stage is probably of some importance. I would recommend a state of benign neutrality and respect.

Neutrality is the secret in avoiding the influence of internal influence coming from one's own convictions, such as suggestion and autosuggestion (as for example when you say to yourself I'm sure this is what's happening). It is the principal enemy of the radiesthesist and can be overcome by using suitable formula, such as: "I am totally neutral," "I know nothing," "This person/other dimensional entity/ fragment is returning to where they originated," or "May they depart in peace and love". Find your formula so that unnecessary impressions take less space on your mental horizon.

This is why it is so important not to linger too long on a clearance. So many ideas can jostle in the mind space just when they shouldn't! Stay in the light.

As in radiesthetic practice, when formulating a question, the gravest error one can make, because it will invariably alter the answer, is to have the slightest belief in knowing what the answer is. Keep a blank mind, with absolutely no intention.

No matter how pure an intention is, it has originated in the mind of the person, that is a cold, hard fact. I am convinced that in the domain of spirit release, it is not a matter of what one human wants or does not want, otherwise there is little difference from the world of magic where one is employing unknown forces to achieve what ONE wants, it is what the entity <u>needs</u> as a function of the guiding Superior Intelligence. Despite all the talk nowadays about intention being key, remember the old proverb about the path to hell….

It is not coincidental that the organ most commonly impacted among therapists, are the kidneys. In Traditional Chinese Medicine, the understanding is that it is the heart which entertains thought; the heart is the pivot between the spiritual and mental faculties, the calm centre of life. It is heart-mind complex which, if not kept in check, goes round and round in overthinking mode (melancholia). However, when a winning number is drawn, and you are sure that the thought is the right one, ideal for the situation and just what the doctor ordered, it heads over to the spleen, the organ of intention, and the thought matures with a plan formulated as to how to implement it all and bring it to fruition. Intention comes about thanks to a certain process, in much the same way as the spleen assimilates whatever is put into the stomach, intention is developed as a function of what is available and even possible. When the end product has been prepared, the thought-project then moves over to the kidneys, where will kicks in, for without will you achieve nothing. It is only when the will is set in motion that things can actually start happening, until then it is all theory.

Incidentally, there are two enemies of the spleen from the physiological view – ice and MSG. There is every reason to believe that our capacity to develop intention has been progressively undermined since the 1960s. At that time iced drinks became popular and even fashionable, only the British were laughed at for drinking their beer warm! But far more insidious was the introduction of monosodium glutamate (MSG) into the food chain. MSG is now concealed as an ingredient under fifty or so different names in the majority of industrial foods and almost all drinks, and unwittingly in so-called natural products. MSG is a neuro-toxin and creates addiction, it is probably the first of these two properties which paralyzes the spleen from functioning. It becomes easier to understand the general apathy which has overtaken society at large when viewing the subject in this light. Naturally, there is much to be gained by an awareness of this, and even more so by careful questioning with the pendulum.

The practitioner would do well to operate in that spirit.

If intention is systematically undermined by drink and foods that sabotage that vital component of the human and animal life-process, serious effort is needed to offset that demolition. The residue is also feeding into the earth where the filtering process is most probably affecting Nature too. Obviously, we can only work on ourselves to improve this, but to do that we must be aware of what we consume and try to discriminate.

Whilst relief from suffering is not guaranteed as a result of release, solace can definitely be found. It is not our role to play at the Superior Intelligence.

This brings us on to another of those subjects where the individual intuition and confidence will most probably be the right guide.

OTHER-DIMENSIONAL ENTITIES

CHAPTER 15
PROTECTION

Talisman, pure light, angels, prayer, mantra are some items of a long list where you might find your personal salvation. My preference is for the Atlantis Symbol.

In my opinion, the most efficient form of protection, and perhaps the world's oldest "magical" geometric form to have reached our modern age, is the Atlantis symbol, and it is a very powerful one too. It is powerful in what it can achieve with regard to protection of a quite specific kind, but it is only effective if the design specifications are respected in its construction; otherwise, it serves little or no purpose. Great attention must be paid to the geometry, proportion and construction.

We know nothing about its origins, so theories and rumor abound.

Using radiesthetic procedures, however, it can be established that the combination of the geometric patterns and forms making up the Atlantis symbol creates a magnetic field with a surprising strength and radius, and so has an effect on harmonizing telluric energies, but no shield against cosmic forces, EMF, or radiation. Basically, that means that the effect can be used as protection from a large number of magnetic forces, both known and unknown influences, defending the wearer from energy originating in the earth. That is why it is especially useful as defense against harmful intention, providing protection of a psychic and mental nature. Generating magnetic energy as it does, it also boosts the vital force of the wearer.

The Atlantis Symbol

In its ring form:

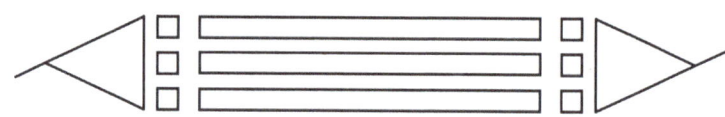

Using radiesthetic procedures, however, it can be established that the combination of the geometric patterns and forms making up the Atlantis symbol harmonize telluric and cosmic energies, but offer no shield against cosmic forces emanating from the sun and universe, nor EMF or radiation. Basically, that means the effect can be used as protection from a large number of magnetic forces, both known and unknown influences, defending the wearer from energy originating in the earth. That is why it is especially useful as a defence against 'psychic attack', 'black magic', harmful intention of both human and mane, providing protection of a psychic and mental nature. It functions on a permanent basis, 24 hours a day with a sphere of influence measuring approximately 2.5 metres around the wearer. The symbol generates a magnetic energy and boosts the vital force.

The overall pattern produces a magnetic field, projecting a negative magnetic polarity in the axis of the centreline for a distance of 60 cm or so in both directions, depending on the energetic makeup of the immediate environment (including the wearer's magnetic field). The geometric forms are of great importance in creating the polarized field, with each component playing a role. The proportion of the pattern in relation to the overall field is of great importance, to the extent that if it is not respected, the ring serves no purpose at all. The central point of the three parallel lines is neutral with the outside edge of the ring producing a positive magnetic polarity. The groove connecting the two holes on the inside of the ring ensures the complete loop of the magnetic circuit. The ring does not generate vital force but, I believe, conveys it on the magnetic phase of the energy field created by the ring.

The Atlantis symbol gained quite a reputation following the excavation of Tutankhamun's tomb by Howard Carter in 1922. He reputedly owned a sandstone ring with the symbol engraved on it, and according to the rumour put out by an Italian journalist on the scene, it was the panacea to Tutankhamen's curse, which struck down all other members of Carter's team in untimely deaths.

In actual fact, this was nothing more than a sensational piece of journalism which holds the public imagination to this day. The only person who died in the immediate aftermath of uncovering the tomb was Lord Carnavon, the expedition's sponsor. He was in Egypt on the advice of his doctor, who instructed him to sojourn in a dry climate such as Egypt following a car-racing accident in England that had seriously damaged his lungs. He died following a blood infection after he had nicked a mosquito bite while shaving. This was not quite the type of news to make headlines.

Carter was an active trader in Egyptian artifacts during the time he was in Egypt, and he had probably found the ring at a dig or marketplace. Careful research into what happened to the team members reveals that nothing untoward happened to any of them. Carter makes no mention of the symbol in any of his books, and careful inspection of photos of him at the time, reveal no presence of the ring on his person.

The much more authentic story of an Atlantis sandstone ring originates in France, with our two celebrated radiesthesists introduced above, André de Bélizal and Leon Chaumery. De Bélizal claims that the negative green frequency took the life of Chaumery by dehydration — one of the effects of this specific energy form as seen with mummification in a pyramid.

The great-grandfather of de Bélizal's wife, the Marquis d'Agrain, was one of the savants on Napoléon's expedition to Egypt in 1798-1801, during which time he "found" a sandstone ring with the Atlantis symbol engraved on it. As chance would have it, that same ring was in de Bélizal's desk drawer during his period of experimentation in the 1930s and 1940s, and, as he claims, thanks to the ring he was spared the dehydration problem that took the life of his colleague.

It is practically impossible that this was the same ring as Carter's, given that de Bélizal's ring had been a family heirloom since the early nineteenth century and was still with the family as late as the 1970s.

Ever since discovering the symbol, I have used it in the form of a ring, a belt and a paper symbol, on myself and others. An important thing to remember in this uncharted world we navigate is that there always someone or something more powerful than yourself – no matter how well you are protected, no matter the purity of your heart.

Please excuse me if I recount another experiential anecdote, but the purpose is to give an example of how little we know, and how submission to the will of the Superior Intelligence is the only salvation we can hope for – perhaps the best form of protection.

A few years ago, I was called upon to help resolve a situation that had developed amongst three people who were starting a well-being centre in Bangkok. I had been acquainted with one of them, a Japanese woman, for several years, and it was at her request that I – innocently/naively – consented. Suspecting geopathic stress to be the culprit, I worked on the premises, as also the homes of those concerned. All went well for several weeks until an urgent call for help was raised by one of the other partners. An extremely ugly situation had developed with the blame being laid firmly on the head of the other by each of the three women. I was left in the distinctly uncomfortable position of finding the culprit(s). In retrospect, wisdom would have dictated that ego struggles like that need to be resolved by the antagonists themselves, as indeed finally happened, but not until after my intervention and the incurring of some very intense antagonism of my erstwhile 'friend', and severe misery for me.

In what I can only express as a psychic attack, I went totally blind for three hours, not knowing if my sight was to return or not; for maybe two or three days my magnetic polarity was reversed, a very uncomfortable – to say the least – experience, although I can now better sympathize with menopausal women, for that is what happens to them. I discovered this by using my pendulum over either hand, and the normally right-rotating pattern for the right hand was inversed, and *vice-versa* for the left hand.

This happened despite wearing an Atlantis ring on my hand, and an Atlantis belt around my waist.

Only after total rest, lying quietly on the bed, thinking of nothing, or as little as possible did my sight return. Twenty minutes in the orgone accumulator, twice a day for three or four days, helped restore a modicum of normality.

The only conclusion that slowly made its way onto my horizon was that my intention to help was substantially weaker than the <u>will</u> that was opposing my action. Intention is a subtle form of desire, and desire is intention transformed into will, a trouble-maker at the best of times. Another fact that I learned, rather understood, later was that my 'friend' had been trained in some obscure sect as a medium, and although she was reluctant to be doing that, being of that disciplined national group (Japan) allowed no discussion, she in all probability knew a great deal more about directing and focussing thought than many, and my goodness she was competent as I learned to my cost.

Although not exactly a method of protection, there is a very useful *mudra*, used by the fingers of the hand not holding the pendulum, which apparently lets you offset the 'magic' miasma. Bring the tip of your little finger ("pinkey") into contact with the tip of your thumb, and ask the question again. This time you will overcome the possible obstruction to the truth

In Charles Kreb's Learning Enhancement Acupressure Program, this type of *mudra* is a standard and constant practice.

This simple gesture works well, and the image of the surprise on the face of a BIDORT (Bi-Digital O-Ring Test)-practitioner friend some years ago is still with me. I had asked him to check the strength of the Thumbkey compared with the regular hand position. It has surprising qualities.

OTHER-DIMENSIONAL ENTITIES

CHAPTER 16
HISTORIC CHARACTERS SHOWING OTHER DIMENSIONAL ENTITY PRESENCE

Some famous names were mentioned above as being of the violet colour. In the interest of us all, I asked some time ago those other dimensional entities present in those personalities, or still in their environment, if they were happy to move on. I believe they all went to the light, as you will probably discover on calling up an image of those various characters to ask what is their colour. Those entities are/were not working for the benefit of humankind, and they were quite happy to cease their activity, and move to the light where one can assume their evolution (or salvation) is better assured than under the sordid influence of the evil currently afoot. It would be a good idea for any practitioners reading this to consider doing the same, there is a lot of misery and some can be perhaps easily removed. Such action is the least one can do as a human if one aspires to harmony.

This is in all probability a factor found in the repetition of history. There must be a controlling force behind the misery inflicted on humanity on such large scales as is the case most of the time, but especially in major conflicts – a black magician or group for example. But at a certain stage in the total destruction, there is nothing to check the dynamic until all the energy is dissipated. It is what we saw happening from 1895 until the end of the second world war, namely a well-organized segment of an evil establishment, initially set up in Britain before assuming a trans-national façade, imposing its will on human society, which is incapable of resisting what it cannot recognize, and as a consequence collapses, dragging other societies down in its wake, until such time that many of the world's nations are aflame, exhausted, demoralised and destitute. While a few individuals/families profit financially and probably become more magically powerful.

To develop a little further on this 'black colour' and without overly dramatizing, I think it is perfectly justified to state that human egocentricity has bloomed in recent centuries, particularly in western cultures where ever since the Reformation, the governing structure of society has been eroded. This is merely to say that due to the western lack of morality, compared to the Hindu or Confucian ethic, it has been progressively easier for people to get away with things that would not have been accepted by the majority a few centuries ago. When one combines this removal of restraint with the irresponsibility we entertain with regard to our well-being and employment, it is scarcely surprising that it is every man for himself.

Energy apparently knows neither right, nor wrong. It is a force that works on king and pauper alike. We access that force quite readily in our everyday activities, by thinking, by breathing, by metabolizing what we eat and drink, by sleeping, and so on. Quite with what consequences is another matter, but in some form or another we all, human, animal or plant, participate in sharing this life force. Is it stretching the imagination too far to believe that the aggregated energy force can be focussed and channelled to good or bad, god or devil?

Is it not what we do when forming a desire? You work, materially or psychologically, towards an objective in order to achieve it. If we were materially unable to accomplish our wants, we would probably have given up on desires a long time ago.

The thin line between what is good or bad seems to depend on the quantity of people who benefit, as opposed to the number who find themselves at a disadvantage. Obviously, the individual knows whether their action is altruistic or egocentric. It could reasonably be said that everything we humans do, is egocentric. And this is where the idea of a scale comes in. From 0 to 10, zero being weak, 10 being strong. In the same way, how black is a person? As a rule of thumb, I consider a score of 6.5 as the cutoff point, anything above that, it is best to steer clear of the individual. Below that median, they are still determined to get their way, so best shunned.

In an attempt to define this scale with a succinct description as to what and how:

1. Ego and what I want
2. Ego first and foremost
3. Manipulation without compunction
4. Sophisticated veneer concealing rather sordid characteristics
5. Perversity
6. Bandit, loose cannon
7. Black arts in progress – danger
8. To be avoided, highly dangerous
9. To be avoided, highly dangerous and not confronted
10. Evolved black arts, to be avoided, highly dangerous and not confronted

There is a common thread to history which is rarely, if ever, pointed out. The sequel of events that forms history, as recorded by humans, is most often determined by the actions/desires of an individual. The results, of the events that get into the history books, have a huge impact on humanity and Nature, but we tend to forget how those events were caused by the will of just the one individual.

Does the strength of the will of the individual in question impose on the collective will? It would seem to be a possibility especially if there is absence of any form of will opposing that of the person. That person's determination risks prevailing if there is not a resolve of greater and fixed strength if such an event is meant to be. But if the individual is controlled by a small group of concerted black magicians with a definite agenda, then any collective effort can be confounded and the agenda remains concealed.

Basically, we underestimate the power of applied thought, especially when it has assumed will, for that is where they are coming from, a very well defined and applied determination.

OTHER-DIMENSIONAL ENTITIES

It is when working with people of this sort that one needs protection. Without evoking the possibility of disembodied spirit entities who work at the beck and call of their master to accomplish their nefarious ends, the sheer force of the 'black' person's determination can be deflected by, for example, the Atlantis symbol.

What matters is the need to find a way to deflect the directed energy. Nature appears to be generous enough to deal with the force once diverted. Which just demonstrates once more how little we understand, or are even able to grasp of what's going on!

What is rather vaguely referred to as black magic could be considered as the excessive use of the life force in a single-minded effort to achieve one's personal objectives. When practiced in ritual form, it is seemingly reinforced with the years of intention built-up behind the scenes, and it becomes very convincing. In my practice, this kind of magic often raises its head and is cause for a lot of head-scratching, rethinking and stress. While there seem to be a number of counter-acting measures, the solution invariably needs to be found via the notion that 'all is one', so rather than confront the force – obligatorily stronger than yourself – which thrives on fear and hate, one has every interest to find common ground, that can only lie in the domain of energy and its manifestation of desire. That common ground, I believe, is concealed in the craving (a warped form of love) of the magician, and the minions he/she employs (they are in this worldly domain having failed, for one reason or another, to move to the unity of existence at the time of their physical death).

Clearly, one does not go and knock on the magician's door to suggest a parlay. So, one has to deal with the daunting energy forms, or entities when they move into your space. Without going into the multifarious complications that such encounters involve – and every time is different – the aim is to come to grips/terms, and adopting a page from the Kahuna tradition, convince the beast to change its spots, or something along those lines!

There is one final aspect of this work which deserves some attention, and that is release en masse.

CHAPTER 17
MISCELLANEA

Wherever other dimensional entities congregate, whether it is in spirit houses as one finds in parts east, some lonely glen in the wilds, the dungeons of a chill castle, their one-time hearth, …. They seem to attract others, and although we shall probably never know the whole story, they appear to be open to the idea of release on a large scale. There is no difference in the action of the specialist pendulum between individual and mass send-off, so it can be used effectively in such cases.

Sites of battle, strife, famine, destruction of all sorts are often the places where entities are still present. The shock from life ending so abruptly would appear to modify the process more easily approached when dying in a more peaceful manner, but that is my imagination speaking. Nevertheless, spirit presence is very often due to events occurring in the past in such areas.

It is perhaps idle curiosity to ask "How many?", but if one is living in that geographic region, one can acquire a better understanding into the group mentality of the culture, and therefore information which might help one's method of both thinking and working, in addition to the historical perspective.

Of the avenues to be explored so as to gain a better understanding of the elusive relationship between spirit and matter, I would add this final section.

As you have gathered from the above, I am inclined to intellectualize, but I'm working at it, trying to allow more room for the heart and will finish this brief essay on a metaphysical note taken in part from my book, *The Way of the Skeptic*.

Although we shall never be certain what *neter* (*neteru* in the plural)

OTHER-DIMENSIONAL ENTITIES

meant for the Egyptians, one thing seems highly probable: they represent principles, components of energy that make up the cosmic and earth relationship, or harmony. Like any principle, they are an inherent, governing idea specific to form and/or function; there is no question of divine, semidivine, or human capacity here, simply a statement of natural fact.

In *neter*, one can find a link between spirit and matter.

Assuming, as I do, spirit to be one, all-pervasive, and the substratum of existence, consciousness, and love — the source of all materialized forms — it is an easy step to assume further that matter has no existence outside of the spirit apart from a sense-induced appearance in conformity with our mind function.

That allows individual experience (sense-originated and mind-filtered), confirmed by intuition (intelligence of the heart), to be free of hypotheses, any notion of cause and effect or scientific theory, making the latter constructs totally superfluous and thus freeing the way for *neter*-refined perception. Taking things out of their context may be a convenient way to achieve an academic cause-effect opinion with regard to makeup and function, it is not an intelligently sensible way to do it, because the wholeness of Nature is exclusive and allows for no separation.

What actually happens when we analyse something? We remove it from its context, subject it to a scrutiny that is generally far removed from its normal (natural) environment, and in so doing not only separate what we are trying to understand but modify that very environment. Modern physics demonstrates this process.

We may learn a lot of facts but not about the "something" we originally wanted to examine, because very rapidly we learn that the "something" is so closely related to all that is happening in its vicinity, if not further afield, that we end up looking at a separate entity, quite apart from the original or what we believed that to be.

Modern science does not perceive this situation because it is determined to discover how things work at any cost, and either conveniently ignores or forgets this wholistic principle in a sincere attempt to reveal what is concealed.

Many scientific discoveries have come about by accident rather than as planned. Perhaps not being fully aware of what one is doing sometimes results in something that WORKS, even if it is not in the precise domain in which the revelation was intended. This is very much in keeping with what little I understand and what Nature has shown me, because there is no discovery here in this world, merely a revealing and application of what is and has always been.

Regarding things in such a way stands the idea of intention being all-important somewhat on its head, which is where it deserves to be, as that viewpoint is one more manifestation of the misplaced idea of human supremacy. Energy is not mechanical until it is materialized, when its movement becomes mechanical. Similarly, *neter* is not operational, but it defines the operating method.

The trick is being consciously in synchronization with this "state," very much — I believe — in line with the affinity found in most esoteric traditions, namely the harmony of unity or love.

Nature sorts everything out by establishing harmony. Dostoyevsky has one of his characters in *The Idiot* say: "Beauty will save the world." Beauty is an attribute of Nature, so that makes perfect sense. The affinity of existence-consciousness-love shared by one and all creates this natural order, which is quite beyond our understanding as ego-driven human beings.

Nature is very much alive and constantly striving to stay that way, using forces that we are unable to explain, with which we are totally familiar yet quite unable to grasp in terms of how they function — for instance, electricity and magnetism, amongst others. We humans feel safer when a logical explanation is provided, for the simple reason that limits are imposed and it is then easier to control our fear of the unknown.

That we are unable to recognize this is one thing, but knowingly refusing this evidence due to apprehension or denial of our own shortcomings not only prolongs the *status quo* but risks hampering our well-being by negligence…

The thrust of the above could be resumed as follows: only when we consider these unseen but apparently real domains from a wholistic basis, i.e. from the stance of the fully integrated human faculties of logic, intuition and senses, are we able to achieve an authentic personal experience, which remains to be backed and supported by verifiable scriptural authority, worthy of trust, and shared by other agenda-free humans.

CONCLUSION

We, as humans, do not know very much in general about the functioning of what we call life (some might say that is an exaggeration – we know nothing!). Our esteemed sciences are fundamentally flawed from the wholistic viewpoint, as they are all based on separation and differentiation of the components; life does not seem to operate in compartmented branches of activity. Not that you are expected to adopt such an all-inclusive stance, however in the spirit domain – the subject here, it is nigh on impossible to assume any other view if one hopes to reach any kind of satisfactory understanding, let alone explanation. There are things we perceive with our eyes, but so many more that we will never see (a blessing perhaps); one only has to consider the question of the miniscule spectrum of the Hertzian frequency range that we perceive and discussed above to appreciate that fact, and its conclusions.

Consequently, there are no rules, nor defining reference works to guide us, and it is unlikely that there will be until we reach some kind of agreement as to what is going on energetically in the broadest possible sense. Paul Dirac suggested a 'sea of energy' back in the 1920s, but no one seemed to follow up in the domain of physics, whereas those involved in the field of 'energy' (in its widest sense) know that life displays a vital force (whatever you call it, the name is of no significance, it is), which is not only everywhere but able to entertain all manner of conjecture. So, any guidelines in this ambiguous matter might be welcomed, and that was my objective here.

It would be particularly gratifying if this essay were able to remove some of the apprehension so often encountered as soon as we broach the delicate subject of death. By calling on experiential, textual and cultural reference, especially the traditions of China and India, which form a large part of the basis of my theoretical practice, let's look at what little we 'know', and perhaps de-mystify and simplify the phenomenon of the 'spirit world'. The wholistic process employed involves sifting through experience, rather than any kind of quantifiable measurement of how or why, for the simple reason that anything hidden or occult can only be inferred, never proved. If understanding can be consolidated into conviction or firm belief, then one is better prepared to deal with the challenges to be met. Only by knowing, as in gnosis, through personal experience is one able to discover the ultimate basis of life rather than merely explaining the phenomena that arise.

Appendix 1
SOME INPUT FROM CHINA

3 Hun(s) and 7 Po(s) (三魂七魄)

As recorded in an ancient Taoist text 云笈七签 **(Yun Ji Qi Qian)**

3 Hun 魂 and 7 Po 魄

Three Hun

胎光 (T'ai Kuang) – The Original Spark, this might be considered as the animating spark of vital force which commences for a human whilst in the mother's womb as a foetus. The spark, so to speak, in its naked simplicity which remains with the human for its entire existence, until death. There is a Taoist text which says: "When T'ai Kuang is lost, a person can still absorb food and water, but is considered already dead, a walking dead."

胎 (T'ai) – the pregnant womb; to commence. 光 (Kuang) - light, lustre, glory.

爽靈 (Shuang Ling) – The Vivacious Spirit, is that bright energetic force which exists in humans and animates the intelligence – the ability to communicate or connect with every thing, whether apparent or not. It is allegedly said that children who are mentally handicapped or autistic are due to a loss of Shuang Ling. I would further add, as confirmed using a pendulum, that curse or inserting certain harmful substances into the body can also result in the Shuang Ling quitting.

爽 (Shuang) – alert, sunny, lively, cheerful 靈 (Ling)- spirit or energy of a being, elevating power.

幽精 (Yu Ching) - The Essential Prison, whereby being trapped in a physical body teaches you to overcome the earthly addictions of lust, the chaos of thinking, depleting one's energies, by aspiring to spirituality, discerning between good and evil, establishing love for one and all, nourishing your vital force by careful control of quantity and quality of food and water – thus maintaining harmony. This *hun* also determines the individual's sexual orientation and sexuality.

幽 (Yu) – Darkness, quiet, prison, hell. 精 (Ching) – The essential part; essence, spirit, semen, skill.

The 7 Po(s)(七魄)

吞賊 (**T'un Tsê, T'un** - to swallow up, engulf. **Tsê** – thief, to ruin or chastise) - Engulfing Thief. Eliminate harmful substances at night during sleep, a function of the immune function.

尸狗 (**Shih Kou, Shih** – corpse. **Kou** – dog) - Corpse of Dog. Remain alert when sleeping, instinct of self-preservation.

除穢 (**Chu Hui, Chu** – to take away, deduct. **Hui** – unclean, to defile) - Remove Filth. The autonomic action of cleansing the metabolism.

臭肺 (**Ch'ou Fei, Ch'ou** – to stink. **Fei - lungs**) - Smelly Lung. Respiratory regulation throughout the life of a human.

雀阴 (**Ch'iao Yin, Ch'iao** – sparrow. **Yin** - *Yin*) - Yin of Sparrow. Regulation of the reproductive function.

非毒 (**Fei Tu, Fei** – not. **Tu - poison**) - Not-Toxic. Scatter evil deposition, such as tumours, etc.

伏矢 (**Fu Shih, Fu,** to hide. **Shih,** dart, arrow) - **Concealed Arrow.** Dispersion of toxins in the body.

THE END

www.ingramcontent.com/pod-product-compliance
Lightning Source LLC
Chambersburg PA
CBHW042258280426
43661CB00097BA/1182